Health
and
Medicine
in the
Anabaptist Tradition

Health/Medicine and the Faith Traditions

Edited by James P. Wind and Martin E. Marty

The series Health/Medicine and the Faith Traditions
explores the ways in which major religions
relate to the questions of human well-being.
It issues from Project Ten, an interfaith program
of the Park Ridge Center for the Study of
Health, Faith, and Ethics.

Barbara Hofmaier, Publications Coordinator

The Park Ridge Center
is an affiliate of Advocate Health Care.

The Park Ridge Center
211 East Ontario, Suite 800
Chicago, Illinois 60611

Health
and
Medicine
in the
Anabaptist Tradition

CARE IN COMMUNITY

Graydon F. Snyder

TRINITY PRESS INTERNATIONAL
Valley Forge, Pennsylvania

Trinity Press International, P.O. Box 851, Valley Forge, PA 19482-0851

Library of Congress Cataloging-in-Publication Data

Snyder, Graydon F.
   Health and medicine in the Anabaptist tradition : care in
community / Graydon F. Snyder
      p.   cm. — (Health/medicine and the faith traditions)
   Includes bibliographical references and index.
   ISBN 1-56338-120-6
   1. Anabaptists—United States. 2. Health—Religious aspects—
Anabaptists. 3. Medicine—Religious aspects—Christianity.
4. Anabaptists—Doctrines.   I. Title II. Series.
BX4933.U6S68 1995
261.5'61'088243—dc20   95-16094
                                                                   CIP

Printed in the United States of America

95   96   97   98   99   5   4   3   2   1

To the many faithful
who, by the way they lived and died,
mirrored hope
for the next generation

Contents

Foreword

"God chose what is weak in the world to shame the strong; God chose what is low and despised in the world, things that are not, to reduce to nothing things that are, so that no one might boast in the presence of God" (1 Corinthians 1:28 NRSV).

For the first time in this series of fourteen books, I open the foreword with a biblical text. The people being introduced would be pleased, and other Christians who know them would not be displeased. Know them well or hardly at all; like them much or little or hardly at all: it makes little difference. The people who make up the communities in the Anabaptist tradition think biblically with special vigor. As author Graydon Snyder says, they have no Luther, Calvin, or Wesley (though one group is named after one Menno Simons); "except for the witness of the New Testament, Anabaptism has no unifying source."

As for the description in the verse from the first letter of Paul to the Corinthians, the Anabaptist tradition would seem to come under its umbrella. As the world counts strength, it is "weak." As the Luthers and Calvins and Wesleys or other powerful leaders of church — and state — looked or could have looked at them, they were "low" and "despised." A book called *Martyrs' Mirror* is the classic of their tradition. Statistically, in most of the world, Anabaptists almost "are not." And the last thing they should be caught doing, even when given a chance to advertise their approach and achievement in respect to health and medicine, is to boast in the presence of God.

If they "are not," or are not visible to most people of power in most places; if their churches are not large presences as are those of Baptists or Catholics, who are they?

Graydon Snyder defines them well, and I do not want to anticipate his plot so much as tease readers into it. Those who are in the tradition, which

ix

means in the United States up to a half million people who share membership or draw directly on its influence, do not have to ask who Anabaptists are. They are likely to learn much here about what their tradition has to offer on provocative issues of our own time. The rest of North America, including Christians in America, should welcome the spotlight Snyder throws on a tradition about which they may well know little.

The question of "who are they?" does connect with "where are they?" Whoever glances at an atlas of American religion might think that this book is a guidebook to pockets of population in "Pennsylvania Dutch" country. Over half the members of the Church of the Brethren live and worship in Pennsylvania, Maryland, and Virginia, near where they settled in the eighteenth and early nineteenth century as they sought refuge and opportunity after Europe offered little of either.

A second cluster, the various Mennonites, are mappable in similar locales, and, with the Brethren, have fanned out and created a thinner spread of settlements in Ohio, Indiana, and all the way to the Pacific Northwest. A third, the Old Order Amish, who are by far the smallest of these three and by far the most familiar to outsiders, are strong, if the weak can be said to be strong, in Ohio, Indiana, Wisconsin, and elsewhere in the Midwest. Only one group of these, their presence indicated by the color yellow on my map (which means only "1–150" adherents in the county) exists west of central Kansas. But thanks to an old Broadway show, *Plain and Fancy*, and a sympathetic film, *Witness*, plus the iconic value of photographs depicting black-suited farm children riding buggies and their parents raising barns, everyone knows these Amish. Still another group to which Snyder gives notice, the Hutterites, hardly show up on any maps; look for them in places like rural South Dakota.

In other words, residents of New York, Chicago, Los Angeles, Dallas, and all other big cities; again, in other words, Catholics, Baptists, Lutherans, Methodists; all of you "powerful" and "high" and "respected" people, you who really *are* somewhere and something — you can forget about the Anabaptists and boast.

Never.

At least not as easily if you read about this distinctive Christian movement and see how it reckons with a tradition. Now it is up to me to suggest why this heritage deserves the attention that Snyder gives it.

For the issues of health and faith and ethics, the main reason lies in the countercultural effects of the Anabaptist movement. Most countercultural impulses come with bluster, become a fad or an object of celebrity, and then fade. Where are the counterculturalists of yesteryear, the bearded dropouts of the sixties? (Look for them beardless on Wall Street, or tenured at prestigious universities.) The Brethren and Mennonites, Amish and Hutterites, come quietly, never become a fashion and seldom acquire celebrity, but they don't fade. Their denominations experience different fates. Thus the Church of the Brethren mysteriously is declining (from about 190,000 at midcentury to 185,000 near its end; from 460 congregations to 420 now), while the Mennonites mysteriously prosper, having grown from about 65,000 then to 155,000 now. The Amish are believed to be growing, but statisticians have to do so much guessing about the size of their communities that no one can be sure. And these denominations have a way of splitting. Though Anabaptists are devoted to peace and reconciliation, they have the same unfortunate tendency to divide that other church groups do. They tend to be peaceful toward everyone except each other when they engage in church fights. But Snyder does not have to concern himself with all that: he is talking about the overall witness of a tradition.

How is it countercultural? Maybe the first clue is in the word *witness*. Many movements spend a good deal of energy in market research, in calculation, in pragmatic politics. But the Anabaptists tend to say that they must simply witness, usually quietly witness, because the call of God demands this, whether the outcome will mean success or whether they have persuaded others to line up with them. Thus their form of witness has produced pacifists through many wars in many nations, and through both world wars many Anabaptists in the United States witnessed their way into alternate service or even imprisonment. They get less notoriety or credit for this than do their better-known cousins, the Quakers; but there they are!

More relevantly, for the purpose of this book, they are countercultural because their approach to understandings of health and illness, care and cure, groping for meaning and coping with suffering and death, is communal. Anabaptists can be cantankerous and individualistic in temperament. But as they read their New Testament, they find its texts committing them to community life. Snyder drops their phrase *mutual aid* with almost wearying frequency, but still it inspires. In a time of excessive individualism, of privatized spirituality, of "pick-and-choose" religiosity, of self-improvised self-cures, these groups — Brethren and Mennonites, Amish, Hutterites, and others — try to make sense of birthing, maturing, and dying, in the context of community. They do this sometimes in ways that can repel others; community can be repressive, exclusive, introverted.

But just as often their ways are attractive and can serve as models for others.

Mutual aid is not where Anabaptist efforts to care and to heal end. These groups have pioneered with agencies like the Mennonite Central Committee or the Heifer Project, efforts that reflect local and domestic concerns but project them into all the world beyond the zones of their own mutual life. Contributing funds to such projects is not sufficient; one is expected to put a body on the line. We all have images of how this is done. Our family recalls a typical instance on a Sunday night at a service station in central Illinois. Next to us was a van with Indiana license plates; around it were several middle-aged men, some of them bearded. They were fueling it, scraping grasshoppers off the windshield, washing windows (inside and out), bustling to get home for work on Monday. Who were they? Where had they been? I remembered that a tornado had touched down in Oklahoma three days before. To ask where they had been was hardly necessary; their answer was predictable: "Oklahoma, to help the victims rebuild."

Simplicity — there's a third key word that courses through these pages. The Anabaptists believe they have simple readings of a simple New Testament. Unfortunately for them, Snyder is a sophisticated New Testament scholar and hermeneutician, which means that he thinks a good deal about the arts and sciences of interpretation. So he knows that they have hermeneutical approaches to the Bible, just as do all others. They select the portions that speak most compellingly to them, and they interpret many passages — for example, Jesus' commands to be peaceful — differently from, say, their "pro–just war" interpreters in majority Christian communions. For all that, their intention to keep things simple, to recall primitive Christianity, to reject whatever stands between Jesus' call to discipleship and his mandate to heal, on one hand, and, on the other, themselves and the people they would serve.

These years Americans of secular and Jewish-plus-Christian descent and orientation read much in Hindu, Buddhist, and other texts that are anything but mainstream in their understandings of the themes that Snyder expounds. Some of these citizens successfully import motifs from such religious traditions, fuse them with their preexisting native and natural Western worldviews, and sometimes even undergo profound conversion with lasting results. Most are informed, sometimes inspired, by these alternatives. One hopes that some of these readers will use Snyder's pages in order to become similarly informed and inspired, even though the author is not trying to lure anyone into the Anabaptist precincts.

We used to play a game among people in diverse faith communities: suppose, for unanticipatable and inexplicable reasons, that your own faith community, religious tradition, or denomination were to disappear; what would you likely find attractive in its place? What would you become? My answer was this: Catholic *or* Mennonite. What sense did that make? Those two terms indicate two poles in the Christian ellipse of witness and experience. One is complex, rich, hierarchical, able to penetrate all dimensions of culture, faithful to one aspect of biblical and traditional witness. The other is simple, primitive, communal, somewhat restricted in its cultural ambitions, faithful to another aspect of biblical and, to a lesser extent, traditional witness.

Fortunately, we were only playing a game. Having to encounter its possibilities in real life (and thus, for me, having to mourn the passing of my own tradition!) is unlikely. Yet the instinct to answer the question the way I did indicates something of how I hope this book works on readers who will not even be tantalized to the edge of commitment, who cannot be teased to consider all the positives that go with the tradition. Snyder hopes that readers will not see Anabaptist elements as constituents of a museum of faith, an Olde Curiosity Shoppe translated to and through Pennsylvania Dutch culture. He believes, and in this foreword I want to indicate assent to that belief, that people far from this tradition will profit from many of its intentions, concerns, and examples. It is a tradition that can counter, supplement, and inform the mainstream versions that have received more notice, versions that are more familiar in the Yellow Pages of the phone book. Anabaptists believe in "mutual aid"; here is another of their contributions, one that would include us non-Anabaptists in the circle of mutuality.

MARTIN E. MARTY

Preface

Although my specific field of interest happens to be New Testament studies, the challenge to write this book on health, offered by Martin Marty and James Wind, was a welcome opportunity. Health and medicine have always been significant concerns for me. Because of my interest in medicine, my role in theological education, and my active involvement in Chicago's West Side, I was asked in 1977 by the board of directors of Bethany Hospital to serve with them on the hospital board. Bethany Hospital was then a seriously deteriorating health facility, sponsored by the Church of the Brethren, in an underprivileged area of Chicago. Eventually Bethany Hospital joined the Evangelical Health System (EHS) and was rebuilt as a part of their network. Working within continuing Brethren health agencies and with EHS, I had every opportunity to see the modern problems of health care delivery. As a result of that experience, and at the request of the Association of Brethren Caregivers, I wrote a study book on medical ethics titled *Tough Choices*. In that study I attempted to address modern health problems from an Anabaptist perspective.

One challenge was to apply the ethic of the Anabaptist "peace position" and its deep sense of community to the difficult problems of modern health care delivery. My conclusions — that the heritage of community leads Anabaptists to a holistic approach to health programs, while the peace position pushes them to think globally about community — are not necessarily prominent in this volume, but they can be found nevertheless. Furthermore, what may appear to the reader as descriptions of Anabaptist attitudes and practices may, from time to time, be my perception of what those are, or ought to be. For example, few Anabaptists would describe retirement homes as I have — as communities free to live counterculturally — though many would agree with the intention. And few Anabaptists would describe conception and birth as I have — as community events — though most understand why I have done it.

The challenge is further complicated by the term *Anabaptist*. Under that rubric I have included primarily three groups, Hutterites, Mennonites, and Brethren, each of which belong to the tradition but in quite different ways. Very few writers have attempted to place under one heading the faith and practice of these three groups on any subject. And certainly no one has tried to unify their approaches to health and medicine. Furthermore, except for the witness of the New Testament, Anabaptism has no unifying source. There is no Luther, Calvin, or Wesley. And even if there were a legacy from such a gigantic progenitor, it would not override the witness of the New Testament and would not determine the direction of the faith community (which interprets the New Testament as it is led by the Spirit). Lacking such a legacy, I had to use inference. It is my assumption that Anabaptists will operate out of a sense of community even though that sense takes on different expressions at different times and places. The inferences in this volume derive from that presupposition.

A word should be said about the chapter titled "The Vision Revisited." My emphasis there on the effect of the Jesus tradition (the faith community's narratives about Jesus) derives from a growing conviction that Christianity adapts to various cultures by means of that tradition rather than the official canon. I was asked, in 1992, by my colleagues at the University of Zimbabwe to put this conviction in writing. The resulting short essay was included in a faculty volume on canon, and I later expanded it for a symposium in Trondheim, Norway. The opportunity to teach at the University of Zimbabwe allowed me to see firsthand non-Western methods of healing. That experience forms some of the convictions expressed in the later chapters of the book.

In writing this book, I have used many excellent sources but have not followed any particular school of thought. Yet though I alone am responsible for the pages that follow, this book is not actually mine. It belongs to the hundreds who have formed me and taught me. I speak for them, though they may not always recognize what I have said.

Eucharistō pantote peri humōn: I give thanks for you always.

· 1 ·

The Anabaptist Vision

The term *Anabaptist* was used in the sixteenth century as a derogatory description of those Christians who participated in what some call a
more radical Reformation.[1] They were earnest Christians who broke with
both the Catholic church and the Reformed church by forming a faith
community based on adult baptism and voluntary membership. Anabaptist referred to the group's practice of rebaptizing persons who, as infants,
had been baptized in those churches aligned with the state (primarily
Lutheran, Reformed, and Roman Catholic). Through study of the Bible
and church history, Anabaptists rejected as invalid the long-standing practice of infant baptism and therefore denied accusations that they were
*re*baptizing. Because of their more radical beliefs, Anabaptists have been
called by some the left wing of the Reformation.

In order to establish the boundaries of this study we begin with the
Anabaptists of the sixteenth century, though actually Anabaptists existed
much earlier, perhaps even from the beginning of the Christian church.

Pluralism in the Early Church

That great historian of the early church Eusebius of Caesarea (fourth
century) collected invaluable material, much of which is now lost, to describe the unity of the Christian church during its first centuries. Without
his church history we would be forced to reconstruct much of the first centuries from between the lines of early Christian writers. While Eusebius
is absolutely indispensable for our picture of the early church, there are
also ways in which he has seriously misled us. Chief among these was the
assumption that the early church was a unified "virgin" church which was
first violated and polluted toward the end of the first century.[2]

The earliest church, in fact, contained many different faith stances. The

1

most prevalent was a belief in the need to choose, to decide between Two Ways: the way of life or the way of death, the way of good or the way of evil, the narrow way or the broad way. The believer needed to know the difference and make the correct choice: "No one can serve two masters; for a slave will either hate the one and love the other, or be devoted to the one and despise the other. You cannot serve God and wealth" (Matthew 6:24).[3]

Also popular was faith in the heroic power of the suffering righteous as found in the Gospel of Mark (8:34–36): "[Jesus] called the crowd with his disciples, and said to them, 'If any want to become my followers, let them deny themselves and take up their cross and follow me. For those who want to save their life will lose it, and those who lose their life for my sake, and for the sake of the gospel, will save it. For what will it profit them to gain the whole world and forfeit their life?'"

Many others became Christians because of a theology which, following the author of the books of Luke and Acts, included all people, especially people who were attracted to the values of Judaism but could not become Jews: "But you will receive power when the Holy Spirit has come upon you; and you will be my witnesses in Jerusalem, in all Judea and Samaria, and to the ends of the earth" (Acts 1:8).

Others, alienated from God by their reaction to a religion of law and judgment, found new trust when confronted with a vision of God in Christ reconciling the world (2 Corinthians 5:19). More Hellenistic types became Christian because they encountered the presence of God in the Christ whose message was expounded in the Gospel of John: "Whoever has seen me has seen the Father" (John 14:9b).

These differing faith systems existed in different parts of the Mediterranean world, and sometimes side by side. Some believe, for example, that the struggle found in the epistles of 1, 2, and 3 John was caused by the Elder John attempting to encroach on some churches of a different persuasion, led by Diotrephes.[4]

Orthodox Christianity did not develop until Christianity became a state church under Constantine (313 C.E.). Only when there was a head of state, with the power to use force, could anyone designate the form Christianity should take. After Constantine we cannot say for certain what dissenting groups continued. We do know they existed. For example, while the hierarchical, orthodox church was developing, a more intellectual, spiritual church (called gnostic, "ones who know") existed in the same areas. Instead of a hierarchy, gnostic churches kept a more democratic organization. Women were not kept in the background but participated fully in the life of the faith community.[5] Eventually the gnostic churches, in competition with the developing dominant churches, became ahistorical, or totally spiritual. Their gospels lost touch with tradition, and eventually they apparently disappeared.

Another major opponent — indeed, perhaps a major candidate for dominant status itself — was the suburban church, which had developed attachment to martyrs. This church was marked by familial fellowship, including meals with the dead. The martyrs became ancestors of the new family. By the third century this suburban group had developed a fairly complete calendar of martyrs' feast days, celebrated in cemeteries, martyria (burial places containing the remains of martyrs), and eventually buildings with columns and a round apse. These "churches" had no priesthood, no altar, no liturgy; they were social and family groupings based on the Christian tradition. By the beginning of the fourth century the suburban fellowships began to create problems for the so-called city churches. Because they were intentionally social in nature, they could, on occasion, become violent. Paulinus of Nola (d. 431) maintained that people were getting hurt because of festive rowdiness. The city churches eventually put an end to all this, and a church hierarchy replaced the martyrs.[6] The fellowship groups were forced into the city, but as compensation they were allowed to place the graves of the martyrs, or their remains (relics), under the altar and continue to mark the calendar of feast days.[7] Even the new church buildings reminded them of the "covered cemeteries" in which they once had worshipped.

Eusebius notwithstanding, then, the church of the first three centuries was pluralistic in form and belief. Dissent to developing orthodoxy could not be traced simply to the presence of a few malcontents; in the case of gnostic Christianity and "suburban" Christianity, dissent was a major faith alternative to the main development. Anabaptists have tended to believe such dissent was there from the beginning and has continued through the centuries.

Later Dissenting Groups

The Unity of the Brethren (Unitas fratrum)

Whatever the history of dissidents might have been,[8] many suspect that the general type emerged over five hundred years ago in Kunwald, Bohemia. The powerful Czech patriot and martyr John Hus initiated the break with Rome, a break that would continue for centuries. Directly related to Hus's protest against papacy and empire was the development of a Czech group commonly known as the *Unitas fratrum,* or Unity of the Brethren. The group, led by Peter Chelcicky, espoused a law of love that repudiated violence and espoused mediation between enemies both at organizational and personal levels.[9] In 1467 the *Unitas* broke with Rome and other radical groups by selecting and ordaining its own ministers. Eventually, under the impact of the Counter-Reformation, the *Unitas fratrum* nearly died out, but not until it had spawned such leaders as Count Nikolaus Zinzendorf and John Amos Comenius. Under the leadership of Zinzendorf it was revitalized in the 1720s as the Renewed Moravian Church and lives on in many nations as a small but influential body.

The Waldensians

Somewhat earlier a merchant of Lyon, Waldo, became convinced that Christians should dispense with their wealth, as the "rich young ruler" of Scripture had been advised: "If you wish to be perfect, go, sell your possessions, and give the money to the poor, and you will have treasure in heaven; then come, follow me" (Matthew 19:21). At first the *pauperes spiritu,* the Poor in Spirit, were welcomed by the church authorities, for they were in no sense heretical. But eventually their life of radical poverty could not be tolerated. In 1184 they were declared heretical. The bloody persecution that followed nearly destroyed the poverty-oriented Waldensians. Fortunately, after surviving centuries of persecution, they were granted religious freedom by Italy in 1848.

The Anabaptists

The pre-Reformation roots of Anabaptism are manifold. For this reason, when the medieval hegemony disintegrated, radical Christianity, as well as Protestantism, appeared in several forms and at several locations.[10] The classic story of Anabaptist origins, however, stems from the early sixteenth century in Zurich, Switzerland. Martin Luther, Huldreich Zwingli, and John Calvin had started reform movements. In Zurich the brilliant Zwingli guided the city toward a reformation, but the town council was not as fast-moving as the reformer himself. In October 1523, Zwingli sought to establish a reformed Eucharist. Discontented both with the Mass and with Luther's moderate changes in understandings of the sacrament, he wished to accent its memorial features and the piety of the communicants over any notions that the bread and wine of the meal somehow "became" the body and blood of Christ. The town council, however, balked at a radical break with the Mass, and eventually Zwingli gave in to their reluctance. Many of Zwingli's adherents were disappointed: they could not understand why a church leader would allow a political entity to determine practices of faith and belief. The disaffection grew. One group of the disaffected, including such scholars as Conrad Grebel (1495–1526) and Felix Mantz (1498?–1527), met on the evening of January 21, 1525, at the home of Mantz. They discussed the implications of learning from the divine word and proclaiming a true faith. According to a contemporary account a sense of angst came over the group, and they prayed to know the divine will. George Cajacob (otherwise known as Blaurock) rose from prayer and asked Conrad Grebel to baptize him with the true baptism. Cajacob knelt and was baptized by Grebel. Each person present then requested baptism from Cajacob. The Anabaptist movement had begun.[11]

The implications of these actions were enormous. That baptismal service of January 21 did more than violate the rules of the Zurich town council. It broke with the medieval unity of church and state. It signaled the beginning of a faith community that had no demographic or political counterpart. The church now became a voluntary organization rather than a religiopolitical entity. Once the dam was broken there was no stopping the torrent of dissent.

The Mennonites

The new movement spread rapidly in Germany, Austria, Switzerland, and the Low Countries. Persecution was intense, and soon the first leaders had been killed off. For the most part the Anabaptists stayed the course of their original intention, but one convert, Melchior Hofmann (1493–1543) predicted an immediate apocalyptic end of the world. While Hofmann was not violent himself, some of his followers, called Melchiorites, were not satisfied with simply waiting for the coming kingdom of God. They received a divine revelation that the German city of Münster would be the New Jerusalem. A religious communism established there reached radical proportions. In 1535 the Münster millennial experience was destroyed when two betrayers opened the city gates to besieging episcopal forces. Ever since, state churches have suspected that the Münster event, with its apocalyptic excesses, might be the logical outcome of the Anabaptist movement. That has not proven true. Touched by the news of Münster, a Dutch priest, Menno Simons (1496–1561), helped pull the discouraged Anabaptists together. The major continuing Anabaptist group eventually took his name as theirs — the Mennonites. In America today there are about twelve Mennonite groups. To some extent they continue earlier European national divisions. The Swiss Anabaptists are called the Mennonite Church. Other major groups are the General Conference Mennonite Church and the Mennonite Brethren Church.

The Hutterites

Many Anabaptist refugees from South Germany and Austria found refuge in Moravia. A leader there was Hans Hut (d. 1527), a follower of the radical Lutheran theologian and leader Thomas Müntzer (d. 1525). The issue of violence continued to plague some elements of Anabaptism. Balthasar Hubmaier led a group which held that the state was necessary and that defensive violence was acceptable. Another group, led by Jacob Wiedemann, held out for complete nonresistance. In May 1527, during a disputation between Hut and Hubmaier, it became clear that their differences were too great for reconciliation. In 1528 the Wiedemann group, following the position of Hans Hut, formed its own community. Holding to the earlier communism, they "spread down a cloak before the people, and every man did lay his substance down upon it, with a willing heart and without constraint, for the sustenance of those in necessity, according to the doctrines of the prophets and apostles."[12]

Hutterians consider this act of communal sharing the beginning of the Hutterite movement. The primarily Austrian group was led, in early years, by the very capable Jacob Hutter, from whom the group eventually took its name. Until this day the Hutterites have lived an Anabaptist lifestyle within communal structures.

Despite the connection with Thomas Müntzer, who was killed for his leadership role in the Peasants' War (1524–25), one cannot say that the first Anabaptists were involved in that popular uprising.[13] Nevertheless, there is a clear relationship. Following the Reformation attack on the Catholic hegemony, the peasants demanded reinstatement of their previous rights to common land, water, and natural resources. Refusal to grant communal access, even by Reformation princes, triggered the revolt.[14] Anabaptists, especially Hutterites, claimed those rights by forming their own communes or colonies as earthly expressions of the New Testament end-time vision. The transforming of the millennial kingdom into an earthly reality set the stage for later socialistic movements in Europe and North America. In other words, the spiritual roots of socialism lie in sixteenth-century Anabaptism.[15]

The Brethren

Once ecclesiastical and political dissent had been initiated by Anabaptists, other Christians also struggled to separate church from state. The movement spread quickly to England where Quakers, Methodists, Baptists, and Congregationalists soon appeared. In many respects the history of dissent ought properly to follow the British line because Baptists and Methodists have become, next to Catholics, the largest Christian groups. On the other hand, German-speaking dissidents, who comprise what we are calling Anabaptists, live out a more radical separation from society than do their English counterparts. One such community arose out of a combination of German Pietism with Anabaptist influences.

German Pietism arose as a protest against mainline scholasticism. One leader, August Hermann Francke (1663–1727), said he would prefer one "drop of true love more than a sea of knowledge." Another leader, Philip Jacob Spener (1635–1705), set up Pietistic support groups or conventicles. Such groups were known as the little church in the big church (*ecclesiola in ecclesia*).[16] In such an atmosphere yet another faith community was born. The nobility of tiny Wittgenstein, north of Frankfurt, Germany, found it advantageous to tolerate religious dissent. In that rare religious asylum a group of ardent Christians, led by a certain Alexander Mack, formed a Pietistic-Anabaptist community. Known at first as New Baptists, or Schwarzenau Baptists, the group, in America, was renamed Fraternity of German Baptists, later German Baptist Brethren, and finally (in 1908) Church of the Brethren. Its members are often simply called Brethren. Founded in 1708, the community of the Brethren shortly thereafter moved to America. There the original Brethren in 1882 spawned yet another group called the Brethren Church.

Characteristics of Anabaptist Groups

Anabaptism has been very difficult to define.[17] The above grouping — primarily Hutterites, Mennonites, and Brethren — cannot be designated as representative of Anabaptists, yet often proposed categories like Free Church or even Believers' Church prove too wide for this tradition. Definitions may finally depend simply on historical descriptions. Yet these three groups do afford an interesting overview of the Anabaptist movement. One branch, the Mennonites, tends to develop social systems as alternatives to the state system. While granting the state its legitimate functions, Mennonites have developed their own programs for education, insurance, pension, and health. On the other hand, the Hutterites tend to deny the validity of the state and historically have been more likely to set up surrogate systems for education, health, mutual aid or insurance, and other services — without granting legitimacy to Caesar. The Brethren tend to believe that the state has a legitimate function and that the state ought to conform to God's will for all. Instead of building parallel or surrogate systems, Brethren tend to seek radical reform. Put another way, Mennonites express the nature of the kingdom of God by dissenting from the dominant society; Hutterites express the nature of the kingdom of God by separating themselves from the dominant society; and Brethren express the nature of the kingdom of God by calling for the realization of divine will within the dominant society.[18]

From this historical overview it should be clear that the churches we are calling Anabaptist have certain elements in common. From a sociopolitical standpoint almost all these elements derive from dissent.

1. *Separation of church and state.* As we have seen, the church was pluralistic from the very beginning. After the conversion of Constantine, the Holy Roman Empire made possible a broad unity under one ecclesiastical roof — the Roman Catholic church. Although the Reformation again offered Christians a choice, it did not promote or allow pluralism to exist within any given political unit. The one religion of the prince, or state, was still the only acceptable religion for the people. When that small group of Zurich dissenters met on January 21, 1525, and baptized each other, the medieval state system was severely challenged. The first Anabaptist group called for a religious freedom that would allow them to carry out the will of God as they saw it, not as any particular political system had decreed.

2. *Adult baptism.* Infant baptism need not go hand in hand with the state church, but historically it has. The child, without its own decision or consent, enters, by baptism, the established society of Christendom. Infant baptism stands in opposition to freedom of choice, to a multiplicity of faith responses, and to an informed decision to join a faith family. For

the Anabaptist these elements are crucial aspects of the Christian faith. Anabaptism takes its derogatory name from its practice of rebaptizing adults who wish to make their own commitment to their faith.

3. *No force in religion.* Separation of church and state automatically requires that neither the state nor any other social structure can force a person to accept a particular faith, or any faith for that matter. Though born of protest against the power of the prince to determine faith, eventually the objection to the use of force became more universal. While they may differ among themselves on whether the state can use force, Anabaptists do agree that *Christians* would not use violence or force to compel others into an unwanted agreement. For that reason Anabaptists are inevitably pacifistic. At the same time they are reluctant to force their faith system on society as a whole. This reluctance, sometimes referred to as "freedom of conscience," deeply affects the social message of the Anabaptist community. For example, many Anabaptists today would disallow abortion but would be reluctant to force that position on society as a whole. Anabaptists would likely opt for a strong Sunday observance but would be slow to enact blue laws. In regard to health practices the belief in "no force" deeply influences Anabaptist programs.

4. *Mutual assistance.* All the Anabaptist groups have set up surrogate social structures. Most noticeable has been the practice of mutual aid. Instead of depending on insurance, governmental welfare, or bank loans, Anabaptists help each other in moments of emergency, disasters, and other times of need. Those who live in Mennonite or Amish territory are well aware of such mutual assistance as barn-raisings. Barn-raisings not only help a member of the community but also serve as important, enjoyable social occasions. Occasionally a popular movie, like *Witness* (Paramount Pictures, 1985), will offer to the public a fairly accurate reenactment of a barn-raising. Such dramatic instances may make good cinema, but less obvious are programs of financial assistance, care for families that have lost major sources of income, care for the chronically ill, communities for the elderly, support for objectors to war, and many others. Health and wellness programs in the Anabaptist tradition stem directly from a sense of mutual assistance. From time to time, in all these traditions, mutual assistance has taken the form of communal sharing of goods. Put another way, all Anabaptists are driven toward communal life, but that often takes the form of mutual assistance rather than common ownership of property.

5. *No oaths and no creeds.* Because of the radical separation of church

and state, the Anabaptist avoids all oaths of fealty. While Anabaptists accept citizenship and generally support the state, they cannot offer un-contested allegiance to any political entity. For someone not raised in this tradition, the depth of this belief may be difficult to comprehend.

It is not simply a rule; it is a deeply rooted attitude. The Anabaptist simply does not think in terms of the *bonum publicum,* nor can the Ana-baptist make the general good the highest priority. Perhaps to the surprise of some, the same attitude reigns in the church as an institution. A church that is identified with the state (often called a mainline church) usually defines itself by creedal statements. Persons who do not subscribe to the creed do not belong or may be declared heretical. In a state church, dis-agreement with the creed was an open invitation for religious persecution or political exile. Some Anabaptists have confessions, though many do not, but none will subscribe to creeds. Objection to creeds does not derive from a difference of opinion but from a belief that no entity, political or ecclesiastical, has the right to determine the faith of a social group.

6. *Communitarian emphasis.* Both the authoritarian nature of the state and the hierarchical order of the church were rejected by Anabaptists. One might point to Anabaptism as one of the roots of modern democ-racy, but probably *communitarian* is a better term than *democratic* to describe this group. Anabaptists do have leaders, but their leaders or-dinarily represent the community. A primary virtue for Anabaptists is *Gelassenheit,* or submission, to the will of God and the direction of the community. *Gelassenheit* is the psychological counterpart of intentional community. In contrast to creedal groups, where a wrong idea can be heretical, among Anabaptists heretics are those with personal ideas.[19] One sociologist, writing about sectarian communities, correctly observes that "a man who reflects for himself is indeed a dangerous man since he asserts a right to personal examination of conduct in an organization which is based on a rejection of the right to establish personal standards."[20] Consequently, individual leadership qualities are not encouraged. Ecclesiastically Ana-baptists speak of "the priesthood of all believers" in order to stress that the charisma does not belong with the prince or the priest. The Anabap-tist movement forms persons who expect a high sense of community and a low sense of individuality. An individual's health or well-being will depend on a high sense of community acceptance. The individual Anabaptist will likely believe that life-and-death decisions are best made in the context of the immediate community.

Faith and Life

The earliest years of the Anabaptist movement are recorded, in part, by a remarkable document, the *Martyrs' Mirror*. Generations of Anabaptists have read the stories of their foreparents, studied the illustrations, and absorbed the same sense of dissent. The story of Dirk Willems is one example:

> In the year 1569 a pious, faithful brother and follower of Jesus Christ, named Dirk Willems, was apprehended at Asperen, in Holland, and had to endure severe tyranny from the papists. But as he had founded his faith not upon the drifting sand of human commandments, but upon the firm foundation stone, Christ Jesus, he, notwithstanding all evil winds of human doctrine, and heavy showers of tyrannical and severe persecution, remained immovable and steadfast unto the end; wherefore, when the chief Shepherd shall appear in the clouds of heaven and gather together His elect from all the ends of the earth, he shall also through grace hear the words: "Well done, good and faithful servant; thou hast been faithful over a few things, I will make thee ruler over many things; enter thou into the joy of thy Lord." I Pet. 5:4; Matt. 24:31; 25:23.
>
> Concerning his apprehension, it is stated by trustworthy persons, that when he fled he was hotly pursued by a thief-catcher, and as there had been some frost, said Dirk Willems ran before over the ice, getting across with considerable peril. The thief-catcher following him broke through, when Dirk Willems, perceiving that the former was in danger of his life, quickly returned and aided him in getting out, and thus saved his life. The thief-catcher wanted to let him go, but the burgomaster very sternly called to him to consider his oath, and thus he was again seized by the thief-catcher, and, at said place, after severe imprisonment and great trials proceeding from the deceitful papists, put to death at a lingering fire by these bloodthirsty, ravening wolves, enduring it with great steadfastness, and confirming the genuine faith of the truth with his death and blood, as an instructive example to all pious Christians of this time, and to the everlasting disgrace of the tyrannous papists.[21]

While it can be helpful to understand Anabaptism as a sociopolitical movement of dissent, most Anabaptists would never think of themselves in political terms. They would define themselves, of course, in religious terms. On the one side, sociologically speaking, the Anabaptists were a voluntary association, but, on the other side, they wished to restore the church of the New Testament. They read the Bible in order to be a model of the earliest church. Their vision is to represent that early church in the modern world. In contrast to mainline churches, which wish to influence society for the public good, all Anabaptists are *restitutionists*. They wish to be like the first followers of Jesus, his disciples, whether or not that serves the public good. While Catholics were concerned about the authority and tradition of the church, and the Reformation proclaimed the priority of the Word, the left wing sought to return to the practices of the early church.[22]

Restitutionism, or primitivism as it is sometimes called, must not be confused with any forms of fundamentalism, or biblical conservatism. Fundamentalism derives from the Reformation doctrine of the Word. For fundamentalists the Word, absolutely identified with the book we call Bible, is literally true and accurate. According to their doctrine of divine inspiration, the Bible is infallible. Primitivism, however, does not concern itself with infallibility or the "one voice" of inspiration. Quite the contrary: primitivists happily embrace the differing voices of the New Testament as a divine permission for the separation of church and state. The slogan "no creed but the New Testament" calls for the authority of the whole New Testament rather than of one specific desired ecclesiastical reading (a canon within the canon). Despite this flexibility, restitutionism takes the New Testament very seriously. With temerity one could say that fundamentalism represents Word conservatism, while Anabaptism represents faith-community conservatism, a conservatism that can appear quite radical at any given time.

The Anabaptist vision begins with a serious reading of the New Testament.[23] The great visionaries of the movement read the New Testament and adapted the life of the New Testament church for their own time. So the visionaries of the church are not great theologians or great organizers. They are "church historians" with a call to "restore" the true church. The vision of the church becomes bright and clear when the community of faith reads the New Testament together and allows the inspiration of the Holy Spirit to guide its members in both their understanding of the text and their action upon it.[24]

In order to understand Anabaptism, and especially its faith, it is necessary to hear what its visionaries have said about the New Testament. One thinks of Menno Simons, Peter Rideman, Gottfried Arnold, Erasmus, Eberhard Arnold, Sebastian Franck — all interpreters of the New Testament and the first centuries of the church who have deeply influenced the Anabaptist vision. We might summarize their understanding of the church under the following rubrics:

Community of Discipleship. Just as the sociopolitical key to Anabaptism can be seen in its dissent, so the theological key to Anabaptism can be seen in its understanding of church. While Anabaptists would seldom reject any orthodox understanding of the church, certain special tendencies are clear. Anabaptists tend not to speak much about redemption, justification, and divine forgiveness. They tend much more to speak of following Jesus, of being obedient to him, of forming communities among those who believe, and of a willingness to give their entire life to Jesus and his church.

Anabaptists read the call of the disciples (Mark 1:16–20) as a call for all of us to leave the vocations of this world and follow Jesus wherever he leads. Indeed we are to follow in the footsteps of Jesus (1 Peter 2:21) even to the cross (Mark 8:34). The community of disciples forms a close-knit fellowship which shares in all aspects of life:

> Awe came upon everyone, because many wonders and signs were being done by the apostles. All who believed were together and had all things in common; they would sell their possessions and goods and distribute the proceeds to all, as any had need. Day by day, as they spent much time together in the temple, they broke bread at home and ate their food with glad and generous hearts, praising God and having the goodwill of all the people. And day by day the Lord added to their number those who were being saved. (Acts 2:43–47)

As a faith community, disciples are members of a body who derive their identity and existence from that body (1 Corinthians 12:12–31). By the action of the Spirit, the functions of the community are granted to particular persons regardless of their prior skills or vocation (1 Corinthians 12:3–11).

Peacemaking. When a community is close-knit, keeping the peace is an absolutely essential function. Put in covenantal or relational terms, one cannot kill, injure, or even attack another person without damaging the community itself. Within the community Anabaptists knew that even hatred or disdain of the other could approximate "murder" (Matthew 5:21–22). If instances of conflict did occur, the members expected that with the help of the faith community, reconciliation would occur as quickly as possible (Matthew 5:23–26; 18:15–17). It was understood that the faith community had the power, acting with ultimate authority, to effect reconciliation (Matthew 18:18–20). Failing that, the community also had the authority to separate themselves from those who could not be reconciled (Matthew 18:18; 1 Corinthians 5:3–5).

While peacemaking and reconciliation are the essential elements of a communitarian polity, Anabaptists did not, and do not, limit their peacemaking to those in the faith community. In the *Martyrs' Mirror*, as we saw, Dirk Willems endangered his own life in order to save his persecutor's life. Though his reward was execution by the officer's superiors, Willems had fulfilled the mandate to be a peacemaker. Anabaptists envision a universal community in the end time. Consequently, though certainly one cannot live in conflict with a brother or sister, neither can one do injury to anyone who belongs to the human community. It is of the very nature of the universal God that one loves not only those who love oneself, but also those who do not (the enemy). That is what it means to be a mature disciple, even as God is mature (Matthew 6:43–48).

Anabaptists take seriously the words of Jesus about conflict with the enemy. They understand that if someone strikes you on the right cheek, you should turn the other, or if someone wants to sue you for your coat, you should give up your cloak as well, or if a soldier forces you to go one mile, you should go yet a second (Matthew 5:38–42). The spiral of conflict can be stopped only if the injured party refuses to participate in an escalating antagonism.

Baptism. The family of Jesus is not coextensive with the family of origin. Jesus made that clear when he denied the authority of his own family and said to those about him, "Here are my mother and my brothers! Whoever does the will of God is my brother, and sister, and mother" (Mark 3:34–35). As an adult Jesus left his family of formation and, filled with end-time expectation, was baptized into the new age (Mark 1:19–24). Jews who expected the coming end time spoke of their futile life in the past as the *old age*. The life ahead of them was called the *new age*. Just as Jesus died to the old age through baptism, so those who follow Jesus will die, through baptism, to their old age and be raised in the new age, the new family of God. The apostle Paul first expressed this when he identified baptism with the death and resurrection of Jesus (Romans 6:1–11). Christians therefore have been buried with Jesus in his death and have been raised as his resurrected body, the end-time body of Christ, the faith community.

To be baptized at birth makes the family of origin and the family of God coextensive. A key element of the teaching of Jesus is to orient us toward expectation of the coming age rather than faithfulness to a heritage of the past. "A man who puts his hand to the plow does not look back." Or people invited to the wedding feast do not stop to care for daily obligations (Matthew 22:1–10). When family of origin and family of God are the same thing, that end-time anticipation has been rendered inappropriate. For Anabaptists the loss of that quality of life created by end-time anticipation is tantamount to loss of the vision itself. What then remains for the Christian is preservation of the past, security for the community, and apologetics for the faith. The Anabaptist critique of the dominant church hinges on this very issue, and adult baptism still remains the key symbol for that vital shift from family of origin to family of faith. The Reformers rightly understood the critical importance of this "second baptism," so it became the major point of contention.

Simplicity. The theological basis for the simple life may be multifaceted, but simplicity characterizes all Anabaptist groups. Anabaptists took to heart Jesus' assurance that if God cares for the birds of the air and the flowers of the field, certainly God cares for us (Matthew 6:25–34). To orient life toward accumulation of goods showed a critical lack of faith, as in the case of the rich man who built more barns:

> Then he told them a parable: "The land of a rich man produced abundantly. And he thought to himself, 'What should I do, for I have no place to store my crops?' Then he said, 'I will do this: I will pull down my barns and build larger ones, and there I will store all my grain and my goods. And I will say to my soul, "Soul, you have ample goods laid up for many years; relax, eat, drink, be merry."' But God said to him, 'You fool! This very night your life is being demanded of you. And the things you have prepared, whose will they be?' So it is with those who store up treasures for themselves but are not rich toward God." (Luke 12:16–21)

Indeed, concern for the things of life could cause the believer to become too attached to the old age (1 Corinthians 7:32–35). Paul suggested it was necessary to suspend (not sever) involvements in the old age in order to live for the coming kingdom (1 Corinthians 7:29–31). Otherwise, involvement in matters of this age could cause debilitating anxiety (1 Corinthians 7:32–33). Paul's words reflect the same concern found in the Sermon on the Mount. It is useless to worry about the things of this life (Matthew 6:25).

Furthermore, the disciple ought to be free of a stationary style of life. Jesus commissioned his disciples to go, two by two, to the villages of Palestine. They were to take nothing with them except a staff, sandals, and one tunic (Mark 6:7–13). The mission of Jesus was carried out by wandering charismatics who had few if any possessions. Like the wandering Cynic philosophers, disciples of Jesus who carried the good news depended on local support. Early Anabaptist historians supposed that Christianity spread rapidly precisely because many of its adherents, carrying with them the gospel and the practices of the new community of faith, could move about freely, across regional and political boundaries. Early Anabaptists, and even modern ones, show the same mobility.[25]

The issue of possessions and technocracy constantly troubles Anabaptists. From time to time they reject personal possessions or refuse to participate in modern technological culture. Consequently all the branches mentioned have experienced communal life, communal ownership, and isolation. At other times, when utopian dreams are dim, they have realized that the transfer of ownership to the community does not solve the problem of possessions.

Oath-taking. In the Sermon on the Mount, Jesus spoke sharply against the taking of oaths. Following the third commandment, the prohibition against using the name of God, the Jesus tradition assumes also that one cannot keep a covenant relationship while abusing the power of God's name or that of anyone else's (Matthew 5:33–37). But even more the very function of oath-taking assumes the possibility of deliberate falsification. The disciple will, with simple speech, use either Yes or No as appropriate.

Parallel to the practice of simple living, simple speech entails far more than refusing to give political allegiance. Anabaptists have assumed that the health of an individual and the health of a community depend on an honesty in communication that eschews complexity of language, doubletalk, deception, and false witness.

Historically the Quakers, one of the historic peace churches (but not strictly in the Anabaptist tradition), have been the most rigorous about language. They refused to alter their language or demeanor in front of their supposed superiors and kept a simple language in their worship. Anabaptists, to this day, look askance at academic language or professional jargon and still prefer simple prayers and sermons to the rich liturgical heritage of the mainline church.[26]

Discipline. Present life in the new age, the end-time age, is not co-extensive with that of the old age. Anabaptists take seriously the ethic of the coming kingdom found throughout the Bible. The Sermon on the Mount was never considered by Anabaptists an impossible ideal nor an intensified ethic designed to bring Christians to their knees before a merciful God. It was seen as an ethic for those living in the new age. This conviction often radically separated Anabaptists from the mainline churches. The faith community consisted of persons who voluntarily

accepted the discipline of a radical "kingdom ethic." In that sense the Anabaptist historians understood the church to be sectarian, that is, there was
a visible line of demarcation between the community of the new age and
the societies of the old.

That line was held by discipline. Because one joined the community of
the new age voluntarily, one could also choose to leave it or be strongly encouraged to leave it. The apostle Paul, for example, strongly urged a house
church in Corinth to return one of its members to the old age (1 Corinthians 5:5). Another case concerned Ananias and Sapphira, a couple in the
earliest church of Jerusalem who had the temerity to falsify their financial
dealings before the community. Their relationship to the community was
terminated (Acts 5:1–11).

Not all discipline meant removal from the new community. We have
already seen that in cases of conflict, mediation was available through
personal arbitration (Matthew 5:23–24) or the help of the church "elders"
(Matthew 18:15–16). But even then exclusion could be the final outcome
(Matthew 18:17).

The sense that something different is required of the disciple is deeply
rooted in the Anabaptist psyche. The law of the state does not determine
the morality of the church. The Anabaptist stands over against society and
insists on some kind of difference.

The Fall. The Anabaptist cannot countenance a Christian state. Ever
since that fateful evening of January 21, 1525, the many children of the
left wing simply do not trust nation-state structures. Israel was a nation attached to the land, but Jesus called his disciples away from that allegiance
(Mark 1:16–20). Early Christian leaders, as wandering charismatics, introduced a considerable paradigm shift. They changed the stationary temple
to a movable body of Christ (1 Corinthians 3:16–17; see also 6:19; Acts
7:48–50): "Do you all not know that you are God's temple and that God's
Spirit dwells among you? If anyone destroys God's temple, God will destroy that person. For God's temple is holy, and you all are that temple"
(my translation).

Their attachment to the land yielded to their obligations to a multi-
cultural city. For example, the mission of Paul ends with his imprisonment
in Rome, the ultimate city (not the promised land), and he announces that
the Gentiles there will indeed respond to the gospel (Acts 28:28–31; see
also Hebrews 13:12–16; Revelation 21:2–4).

Early Christians shifted their allegiance from a specific nation to the
world:

So when they had come together, they asked him, "Lord, is this the time when you will restore the kingdom to Israel?" He replied, "It is not for you to know the times or periods that the Father has set by his own authority. But you will receive power when the Holy Spirit has come upon you; and you will be my witnesses in Jerusalem, in all Judea and Samaria, and to the ends of the earth." (Acts 1:6–8; see also Matthew 28:19–20)

For Anabaptists the church did not fall from grace because of heresy or sinfulness. The church began to fall on October 28 of the year 312, when the Roman emperor Constantine received his vision and was instructed to conquer in the name of Christ. The subsequent Edict of Milan in 313 sealed the fate of the church. The faith once again became identified with a land, with a people, and with specific immovable centers. "The Fall of Constantine" remains today a pejorative phrase among Anabaptists to indicate where the church went astray and what must be undone to restore the faith community to its true New Testament vision.

· 2 ·

Wholeness in Community

The first Anabaptists did not leave us much information about health concerns. That very fact is something of a puzzle. Some have suggested that Anabaptists, who otherwise rejected such medieval religious practices as pilgrimages and the use of relics, reacted against miraculous healings.[1] Although that may be true, more than likely the first Anabaptists derived their medical practices primarily from a folk tradition that utilized folk cures and medicines. Since such therapies were taken for granted, it is not surprising that we do not hear much about methods of health maintenance from writers otherwise engaged in a life-and-death struggle over the nature of their faith.

Healing and health maintenance occurred primarily in the faith community. In order to understand even present-day health practices in the Anabaptist tradition, it is absolutely necessary to grasp the effect of the community in the formation of the individual. Yet unless one is of the Anabaptist tradition, that influence is difficult to comprehend. Consequently some commonly accepted social categories will prove useful.

In recent years social scientists like Mary Douglas and Bruce Malina have made popular a grid that categorizes the relationship of community to individual.[2] They divide societies into four logical types: high individualism–low community; low individualism–low community; high individualism–high community; and low individualism–high community. Because many of us live in a society with values different from those of the close-knit community, a review of the distinctions will help to delineate the Anabaptist type.

High Individualism–Low Community. Much of U.S. society fits into the category of high individualism–low community. In this model the individual shoulders the responsibility for promoting his or her goals; the individualist does not look for support in community or among peers. Such persons do not count on a sense of community to maintain their health; they are much more likely to depend on professionals. Without community protection, lawyers and courts are absolutely necessary. Without mutual aid, financial advisors and insurance programs are needed. Without community health programs, physicians and hospitals are essential.

Some cultural anthropologists have helpfully suggested that for some the human body is actually a microcosm of the body politic. Consequently procedures for maintaining personal health reflect the individual's situation in society.[3] If that is true, then individualists have been effectively separated from their bodies. Anthropologists have defined *disease* as "any primary malfunctioning in biological and psychological processes," while *illness* is the personal secondary psychosocial and cultural response to disease.[4]

The person separated from community has little opportunity to deal with illness and therefore must treat everything as a disease, even though the malfunction may be harmless. In such noncommunities the doctor has the unenviable job of treating the symptoms of illnesses as though they were diseases. The individual lacks a supportive community in which illness can be named and managed. Despite the serious drawbacks of such an individualistic approach, a number of American churches value the integrity and freedom of the individual believer above the formation of a faith community.

Low Individualism–Low Community. Persons in the category of low individualism–low community seek satisfaction in setting up a lifestyle that stands over against society at large. They tend to dress in ways that are not acceptable to the social matrix of which they have been a part. Their personal appearance (hair, cosmetics, hygiene) tends to separate them quickly from those who are socially successful. They are the dropouts of any generation.

Members of this category have little opportunity for strong community. Even if a powerful counterculture did develop, the individual's satisfaction would still be taken from rejection of the mainstream culture rather than involvement in the counterculture.

Counterculturists automatically assume that there is an illness in the macrobody. In their own lifestyle they reflect that illness in one of two ways. On the one hand, they can incorporate the shadow side of society and demonstrate its ill health (poor hygiene, use of drugs, poor diet, disorganization). On the other hand, they can reject society as they see it and opt for a more ascetic and austere approach. They would rely more on folk medicines and folk cures or the use of powerful stones, candles, and similar "new age" cures and prophylactics.

High Individualism-High Community. Persons in this group find meaning in corporate participation. They may be as individualistic as those in the high individualism–low community category, but they hitch their wagons to a corporate star. They believe in corporate life and believe that they as individuals rise or fall with the corporation. Because they are concerned about their own success, they are loyal to the corporation to which they have become attached. They support the macrobody. They help mold corporate policies, and then they live by those policies.

Health for this group cannot be separated from a healthy corporate body. Ill health for individuals arises when they fail to conform to the mores and policies of the macrobody. It would be difficult to distinguish between the problems of the corporate body and the ill health of the individual member. Likewise healthy corporations will have healthy participants. Indeed, such corporations will likely have health programs and health requirements (membership in health clubs, diet-conscious cafeterias).

In America some denominations may take on these characteristics, but one is more likely to find this group in large, seeker-oriented churches like the Crystal Cathedral in Los Angeles, or Willow Creek Community Church, outside Chicago.

Low Individualism-High Community. The fourth group, in which all Anabaptist types can be placed, presents quite a different model. Persons in the low individualism–high community group are members of a community. Their satisfaction in life derives from that membership. Their own individual achievement is not very important, nor does the achievement of the community insure individual satisfaction. Belonging is much more important. One is somebody (and therefore an individual) simply by belonging. The community forms the individual and protects its members.

Individuals will be healthy as long as they belong, whereas ill health derives from rupture with the community. Historic Anabaptists speak of *Gelassenheit,* or submission, as an essential characteristic for community life. Brethren speak of humility. In any case, reconciliation among group members is essential if a healthy group is to be maintained. The major redemptive function of Jesus is to effect such reconciliation.[5] Members submit to these processes of reconciliation, for otherwise there is no possibility of continuing community.

This style of community life does characterize Anabaptists, but it can hardly be limited to those who have been part of this historical movement. Many persons and groups recognize the necessity of community for health maintenance. Americans are especially aware of twelve-step programs like Alcoholics Anonymous which depend on group support for the cure of addiction. They are less aware, perhaps, of Third World health maintenance programs or of base communities, a widespread grassroots development primarily in Central and South America, which also depend on group support. These primary communities, strong advocates of preventive medicine, may well become the Anabaptists of the twenty-first century, as I indicate in Chapter 7.

Communities that consistently represent a counterculture, offer dissent to the dominant culture, or are oppressed by the majority often engage in healing practices not accepted or used by the general population. For example, in the New Testament Jesus cast out demons and made people clean without assistance from the temple officials. Personal healing subverted the official system set up by the Jewish authorities.[6]

In many areas of the world today there are two avenues of health deliverance — the official, often Western, medical help and the community shaman. It is the function of the shaman to administer those rites that restore peace and bring the individual into oneness with the community. The physician and the hospital can seldom do what the shaman does. Indeed, for the shaman healing is not necessarily defined as life-saving. Consequently in many areas of the world the ill person will see the shaman first, and only if that procedure fails will he or she see a physician.[7]

The shaman does not usually represent the leadership structure of a community or serve any administrative function. Normally shamans have had some extraordinary experience that sets them off as healers, and from this they derive their power in the community. In 1992, while living in Zimbabwe, I met a few shamans. One quite successful healer told of a dream (which he apparently did not distinguish from reality) in which he was transported to a high hill and upon awaking was being licked by a wild leopard. After this unusual experience he discovered he had the gift of healing, and at the time I met him he was functioning as a full-time healer. Although some witch doctors may seem quite abnormal in appearance and actions, in most groups the prophet or healer appears to be quite an ordinary person who exhibits this particular ability to heal.

Anabaptist communities differ greatly from Third World areas, but they are similar in seeking health through community wholeness and traditional remedies. Such methods of healing are not highly documented, but most older Anabaptists, if raised in areas densely populated with Anabaptists (especially in regions of Pennsylvania settled by those Germans who came to be known as Pennsylvania Dutch), can tell stories about folk cures, natural medicines, and the power of shamans or powwow doctors.[8] One story about a powwow doctor is told by Irene Schreiber, a shopowner in Union County, Pennsylvania:

> When I knew him, he worked at the AC&F (American Car and Foundry). That was in 1948 and I managed this restaurant, Pennsylvania Quick Lunch, and he used to come in when he quit, at two o'clock, for coffee. And one night...I was limping, and he said, "What's the matter?"
>
> And I said, "I have a corn on the ball of my foot and I can't hardly walk."
>
> And he said, "Come down to the end of the counter."
>
> And then he asked me my name, and of course...my maiden name was what he asked, and when I told him it was Umlauf, he said, "Any relation to Bud?" I said that was my dad, and then he said, "I used to work for Bud." And he said, did I believe in the Bible and God, and I said yes [Anabaptist powwowers normally wanted to know about the person's faith and family connection] and he said, "Well, take off your shoe." And I did, and he run his hand over my foot and said some words under his breath which I couldn't understand, and he said, "Now you can put your shoe on."
>
> And I put my shoe on and I stepped on my foot and I just couldn't believe it because there was no pain or anything.[9]

Fortunately the work of some powwowers has been rather fully documented. The correspondence of one in particular, Christian Eby, of southern Ontario, Canada, has been collected and edited by Patricia P. McKegney.[10] On a Sunday afternoon horse-drawn buggies lined up in front of Eby's house in Waterloo, much like Zimbabweans lined up in front of the prophet's house in Seka. Christian Eby used a variety of remedies: prayer, touching, amulets, laying on of hands, herbs, and natural medicines. On a few occasions he could even cure at a distance.[11] The power of Christian Eby lay not only in his curative abilities but also in his clairvoyance, his wisdom, and his ability to discern what was necessary or possible. Eby attempted to cure such things as goiters, cancer, ulcers, abscesses, eye infections, skin diseases, throat and chest ailments, kidney and bladder problems, stiff joints, heart troubles, rheumatism, bunions, menopause, gallstones, swelling of limbs, mental illnesses, and the all-encompassing "stomach fever."

However we may evaluate shamanism, Eby was successful. For the most part he was a charmer. Many of the letters collected in McKegney's book were requests for him to charm:

> Now I want you to charm for father....Charm him for everything you are able and let me know what you charmed him for and when he should feel a change. What did you charm for him last time. Maybe you better charm him again when he does not know it. You have to believe, haven't you?[12]

One wonders if the writer meant that her own faith could cure her father without his knowledge. In any case she does not seem to believe that Eby had the power to heal without some relationship to the patient. Eby himself made modest claims about his ability to cure: "'I received your letter and will let you know that I have cured some cancers, also have had some incurable ones. It is not certain what will happen in any case. People come to see me. I give a blood purifier and salves.'"[13]

Charmers considered themselves vehicles of divine power. If the ability to charm were passed on it could only be to the opposite sex. In addition to training and information received directly from a shaman, there were manuals available for the potential healer. Anabaptists possessed two such books: *Der lang verborgener Freund* (The Long Lost Friend) and *Sechsten un siebenten Buchs Moses,* translated into English as *The Sixth and Seventh Books of Moses.*[14] The latter book has an ancient history (perhaps dating back to fourteenth-century cabalism, or Jewish mysticism) and contains "charms instructions, admonitions, evocations, explanation and illustrations."[15]

Shamans learned about natural medicines from their medieval manuals, but Pennsylvania Germans apparently garnered the medicinal value of herbs from Native Americans. They brewed sassafras tea to reduce fever and chewed its leaves to create an astringent. Trillium or squaw root was used to ease the pain of childbirth. The bark and root of chokecherry were brewed as a tea to cure colds. Besides offering clients prayers and a healing touch, Christian Eby also sold salves and potions. He sold sarsaparilla, a popular medicine which induced sweating, at $4.00 for a dozen bottles. Some charms do seem strange: "The cavy or common guinea pig was kept by some Germans for the purpose of curing rheumatism....This animal, owing to its cleanly habits, was kept in the house. It was believed that the patient could transfer the rheumatism to the animal by fondling it."[16] Eby sold guinea pigs, but the records do not indicate any harm came to them.

In fact, one owner said his animal was growing fat and the rheumatism itself was disappearing.

Those of us who have never utilized the services of a powwower at least know the pervasive influence of home remedies and natural cures. One of the most popular works ever published by the Brethren, *The Inglenook Doctor Book*, contains many remedies used by the plain people of Pennsylvania during the eighteenth and nineteenth centuries. It is clear that guinea pigs were not the only remedy for rheumatism:

> To one gallon of the best whiskey add one ounce of each of the following roots, bruised: Wild cherry, sassafras, poplar, prickly ash, bitter salad, comfrey, elecampane, rattletop, burdock, horseradish, spikenard, pine tops, golden seal, bittersweet and rhubarb. Dose, one tablespoon before each meal. — Wm. A. Anthony, Shady Grove, Pa.

Or if that fails:

> Take the oldest, rustiest mackerel brine to be had, boil till reduced one-half, wrap the affected parts in flannel and pour on this brine until the cloths are wet. As they dry, pour on more brine. — Lucinda Bailey, Mt. Etna, Iowa.[17]

To be sure some cures seem incredible. Some such unusual suggestions appear even today in Anabaptist circles, though most remedies are simply Pennsylvania Dutch folklore. Laura Fasnacht, a librarian in Union County, Pennsylvania, tells this story about her father:

> My father said when he was a child and had the measles, his mother boiled milk and put something in it and gave him the milk to drink. And when he got better she told him she'd used chicken droppings in it!...He used to tell us that when we were children and we laughed, we thought that was a made up story, you know. But here last month I read in the *Ladies Home Journal* or *Better Homes and Gardens*, one of them, that one of the main sources they use to make vitamins is chicken droppings, that it's an amazing source of B-12. My father should have lived to hear that.[18]

The chicken droppings were no accident. A popular Pennsylvania Dutch ditty recounts their power:

> Haily, haily, hinkle-dreck,
> Bis moriya free iss olles weck.
>
> Heal, heal, chicken droppings,
> By early morning it [the pain] is all gone.[19]

Through the years shamans have nearly disappeared, though occasionally they can still be found. Within the faith community wise counselors (and physicians) continue to have a powerful effect. Folk medicine still persists, but the current Anabaptist tradition leans more toward diet and health foods rather than herbs or potions.

Not all the Anabaptist groups moved in the direction of shamanism. Anabaptists were well aware of the relationship between community and health. They knew also the practice of community healing in the New Testament (James 5:13–16). For reasons not now apparent many Anabaptists failed to avail themselves of the anointing service.[20] It was only the Brethren who formally moved toward community healing by representative leaders. They followed the lead of James 5:13–16:

> Are any among you suffering? They should pray. Are any cheerful? They should sing songs of praise. Are any among you sick? They should call for the elders of the church and have them pray over them, anointing them with oil in the name of the Lord. The prayer of faith will save the sick, and the Lord will raise them up; and anyone who has committed sins will be forgiven. Therefore confess your sins to one another, and pray for one another, so that you may be healed. The prayer of the righteous is powerful and effective.

Brethren found in this passage four key elements:

1. The entire community need not be present for an anointing service. The congregation could be represented by elders (see Acts 14:23). Reconciliation with the elders implied restoration with the congregation.

2. The prayer of the congregation, as represented by the elders, had the power to heal as well as to effect reconciliation and forgiveness. Matthew 18:15–20 was another key text in understanding the authority of the congregation.

> If another member of the church sins against you, go and point out the fault when the two of you are alone. If the member listens to you, you have regained that one. But if you are not listened to, take one or two others along with you, so that every word may be confirmed by the evidence of two or three witnesses. If the member refuses to listen to them, tell it to the church; and if the offender refuses to listen even to the church, let such a one be to you as a Gentile and a tax collector. Truly I tell you, whatever you bind on earth will be bound in heaven, and whatever you loose on earth will be loosed in heaven. Again, truly I tell you, if two of you agree on earth about anything you ask, it will be done for you by my Father

in heaven. For where two or three are gathered in my name, I am there among them.

3. Oil was a traditional medium for healing (Isaiah 1:6), one used by Jesus himself: "They cast out many demons, and anointed with oil many who were sick and cured them" (Mark 6:13).

4. Insofar as the illness was caused by separation from the community (note 1 Corinthians 11:27–32), restoration came through forgiveness of sins (Matthew 5:23–24).

Anointing for healing must have been common in some parts of the early church, but eventually it shifted toward anointing for the dying. By the ninth century it was used almost exclusively for the last rite, or extreme unction. Brethren revived the practice of anointing for healing, but it is not mentioned in official records until 1797.[21] For the last two centuries Brethren have continued to use anointing as a means of healing. In latter years the practice has been expanded to include emotional and psychological problems. Harold Bomberger, a Church of the Brethren executive, describes a typical service:

> The person to be anointed is given opportunity to confess sins or share a statement of faith. Following the declaration, "You are now anointed in the name of the Lord," the officiant adds, "for the forgiveness of your sins, for the strengthening of your faith, and for the healing of your body." A few drops of oil are placed on the officiant's fingers, which are then gently touched to the head of the person three times, once as each purpose is stated. Sometimes the three persons of the Trinity are invoked in conjunction with the threefold declaration of purpose. The prayer concludes with the Lord's Prayer.[22]

For Anabaptists, anointing represents the healing interaction of the individual, the community, and the divine power.

Just as it plays a central role in healing the sick, the community shapes the Anabaptist's definition of well-being.

Most Anabaptists enjoy being Anabaptist because of the tradition's simplicity. Expectations are clear. There are few theological creeds, and in any given age lifestyle expectations are fairly straightforward: no use of violence, separation from the state and dominant culture, traditional definition of family, simplicity in material things as well as lifestyle — all passed to the community by a powerful oral tradition. Though there can be variations, these themes have demonstrated remarkable vigor over the centuries. What could be more simple? Everyone knows what must be done to maintain the respect of the community and stay in favor with God.

Children are raised in a familial, community setting. Community is a day-to-day reality to be sure, but special days are also a particular delight. Christmas and Easter are momentous occasions when all the family comes together. On such days tables are laden with extras like the traditional "seven sweets and seven sours," with delectable foods like chowchow, chicken potpie, chicken corn soup, Lebanon bologna, buttered noodles, mush and pudding, and shoofly pie. Funerals bring back distant relatives and friends. Church days are not much different. Love feasts, the communal meal which accompanied the Eucharist, feature the same Anabaptist foods, and in earlier times would last two or three days. In most congregations the potluck dinners are a marvel to behold. Children participate fully on such occasions. Within the limits of reasonable order, it is understood that children must be a happy part of all these celebrations. It is understood that such occasions create in children a sense of belonging that will never leave them.

After the meal the women and girls move to the kitchen where they wash up the dishes and package leftovers to deliver to shut-ins or families with a particular need. The men take care of the tables, the chairs, and rearrangement of the rooms. While they work, the women tell stories, some of which I recount here as I remember them from the oral tradition that is part of my past.

> Grandmother Ebbinghouse was ninety-six years old. She had three daughters who now lived in other parts of the state. They took turns caring for their mother. She was not much of a problem. She was coherent and could take care of herself. She had made it clear that she did not want any heroic measures when her time came. It came last week. Elizabeth, Naomi, and Dorcas all arrived with their families. It was clear that Grandmother was becoming weak. Everyone gathered in the bedroom. There was one person who was a guest — Dorcas's friend who was a physical therapist. Grandmother's heart began to fail. The guest reached over to rub her back and restore the beat. Grandmother opened her eyes, and uttered her last words: "Don't do it."

At this point there is a pause. Then the storyteller wipes her eyes and continues the conversation:

> Last week one of the sisters passed by the house of Anna Marie. Her baby was due any minute. The sister heard screams from the house. Anna

Marie's first child died in childbirth....(The story stopped. Tears were shed.
The women busied themselves with something else. The story about being
a woman could not go on. Everyone understood. The young women realize
they are sitting in a sacred place.)

Meanwhile, the men switch to the front porch to tell stories and talk
business. The stories built the community and formed the children.[23] Often
the stories were fun. My father loved to tell about the Halloween night he
and his friends pushed over every outdoor toilet in Mexico, Indiana. And
then he would include me — he told about his "straight-A" son who planted
all the onions upside down. Or he told about the time that same son was
asked to wash the car before a big trip back to Indiana: the son opened
the hood of the old Whippet and thoroughly cleaned the motor, and the
family vacation was delayed two days while they waited for the motor to
dry out. What a thorough, bright son! Yes, I was a bit embarrassed, but
I was happy — I knew I belonged. They had a story about me, a story
which would be often repeated. But the stories were often serious. We
heard about a fire at the Redekopp's, and we planned what to do about
it. We heard about the Zigler boy who ran off to Chicago and never came
back. And there was the story about poor Joe.

Joe Yingling came into some extra money and decided to spend it on some
luxuries. He bought a black convertible and parked it in front of his house.
Since he wanted all his friends to know he had a convertible, he left the
top down all the time! It rained last week while Joe was at his shop! There
was a foot of water in the new convertible. (All laugh.)

Such narratives described what it was to be an Anabaptist.

No one ever said what it all meant, but we knew the right thing to do
was help a neighbor in need. We felt the deep compassion and empathy
for one of us in pain. We knew running away from family and community
meant death. We knew being called worldly was a quiet way of saying a
separation had occurred. Somehow we knew we would never be like the
Zigler boy, nor did we want to look worldly and foolish like Joe Yingling.
And then the stories became even more serious. In hushed tones someone told of new martyrs, like the martyrs of old. They told of conscientious
objector Ted Studebaker who, acting as a peacemaker in a Vietnam village, was killed by the Viet Cong. They told of two nurses, working in a
remote village in the Amazon, who were killed by enemy tribes. Somehow we knew physical life was not as sacred as faith, and even one's

life could be given for something very important. And people who made that sacrifice would always be mentioned in hushed tones as if they belonged to the community in some way beyond what most of us could attain. Like Grandmother Ebbinghouse, we knew well-being was far more than being alive.

For most Anabaptists there is no sense of well-being without a kitchen stool or the top step of a porch. Achievements will not replace community. To be sure, like any group of people, there are visible signs of "worldly" success. Some black buggies are blacker than others. Some horses step higher than others. Some plain suits are better cut than others. Some prayer veils display more lace. Some potluck dishes contain more chicken or richer cream. But success does not make one more a member of the community and does not increase one's sense of well-being. Like many cultures the Anabaptist community depends more on honor and shame than on success and failure, or innocence and guilt.[24]

In communitarian societies, honor among members counts more than anything else. Most cultures around the world do value honor more than success, achievement, wealth, or any other mark of well-being. For those raised in such a system, being a member of the group ranks above all other considerations. Being respected within the community represents well-being and a life well lived. To lose that sense of honor can be, will be, a disaster. Consequently few things are more serious than shunning (a system of avoidance designed to shame the deviant). Or, put another way, the loss of that community for whatever reason has serious implications for one's health and satisfaction.

For Anabaptists revelation describes the nature of the community. Compared to other confessional groups, there is less emphasis on revelation as the order of creation, or as the will of God, or even as the Word. Revelation makes known to us the nature of life together. So we know from revelation that reduction of God and persons to things will destroy community. Or we know that killing another automatically terminates relationships. We need not discover these things by trial and error. So well-being is a gift of God as described by revelation in the Bible. For this reason the Bible is studied in the congregation as a guide for communal life more than as a source for personal piety or individual direction.[25]

The complication for Anabaptists arises as adulthood approaches. Children are formed to be part of a close-knit community, perhaps even more so than in mainline denominations. Yet the key to Anabaptism is voluntary association. Young people in the Anabaptist tradition need to back away sufficiently from their own community that their continuing participation in it can be based on a conscious choice. It is not easy.

How does differentiation occur? How can one be deeply involved in a primary community and then make membership in that same community a voluntary action? Does not the description of Anabaptist well-being actually approximate the care for a child given to the total family of God (as in the Reformed tradition)? But it does not. At the time the Reformed, or Presbyterian, child is being confirmed a member of the family of God, the Anabaptist child is being asked to differentiate from the primary community and enter an adult community of choice. Because Anabaptists frown on success, it is not possible to re-enter the community as an achiever or to become an adult by demonstrating one's accomplishments. So second-born believers (a term some use to indicate the paradigmatic shift from the first birth, or family, to the faith community) cannot be acceptable simply because they have somehow succeeded in the world at large.

The other theological strategy for establishing differentiation — law, guilt, repentance, and conversion — raises even more of a problem. Since close communities like Anabaptists depend more on honor and shame than on innocence and guilt, conversional strategies involving repentance are not very useful. Indeed, as means of entering an Anabaptist community, repentance and conversion rank quite low. Guilt before the law does not have the importance of shame in the face of community rejection. This story, told by a Pennsylvania doctor, though possibly exaggerated, may help to explain the issue of guilt and shame:

> A Mennonite young woman had reached her seventh month of pregnancy. She began to show every sign of a premature delivery, even though no medical reason could be found. Her doctor hospitalized her in an attempt to bring the fetus to full term. Another physician (a Brethren) was called in to assist. Reading her case history, the Brethren doctor learned that the woman had undergone two abortions (before her marriage). The doctor (wise in the ways of the Anabaptist community) suspected that guilt for the two abortions was endangering the Mennonite woman's ability to have a normal delivery. So he suggested to the woman's physician that an anointing service was in order. It was arranged. When in the service it came time for confession and reconciliation, the woman burst into hysterical sobbing. The Brethren doctor was pleased. Now she would confess her guilt over the two abortions, and the fetus would be saved. But not so. In fact, the woman did not feel serious guilt over her abortions because her mother had taken her to the abortion clinic. She therefore did not feel she had broken with

her primary community on that issue. The woman confessed instead that
on their honeymoon she and her husband had gone to New York (Sodom
and Gomorrah for many Anabaptists), and on the Sunday evening after the
wedding they had gone to a movie. The child was conceived that very night
on which they had flouted the ethos of their community. The church elder
assured her that she was still acceptable to her faith community despite
this violation. The pregnancy went full term.

Guilt as disobedience can occur, but not as a primary element in the
faith structure.[26] In fact, a strong sense of guilt most likely indicates a shift
from the covenantal nature of the Anabaptist community to a casuistic
legalism. That certainly can happen, but, from a community perspective,
it ought not. Guilty Anabaptists become frustrated because Anabaptists
have no rituals that offer the forgiveness of God. There are no services
of absolution.

How does a young person differentiate from and then rejoin the
community? Essentially the teenager discovers qualities parallel to Anabaptism in some other culture. This happens primarily in school if the
school is a public one. Sometimes it occurs at the workplace. Of course,
there is always the urge among Anabaptists to avoid secular contamina-
tion. In such a case the church furnishes schools and the workplace. On the
other hand, some groups, like the Amish, encourage teenagers to back off
from the community for a time. They are expected to "sow their wild oats"
and then return to the community. The return of the differentiated young
person does not involve forgiveness but acceptance and perhaps even reconciliation. In any case, the major rubric for return among Anabaptists will
be reconciliation (with oneself and the community of faith) rather than
forgiveness of sin, or conversion.

The person who has experienced differentiation in the world at large
often finds upon returning home that acceptance by the primary community creates a sense of self-acceptance also. In that self-acceptance the
adult Anabaptist finds a new sense of freedom — not so much freedom of
choice as freedom from slavery to primary formation. When the young
adult Anabaptist makes a choice to oppose violence, for example, it is
more an acceptance of that value than an attempt to please the primary
community. In that sense Anabaptist congregations are voluntary organizations. Only seldom are congregations composed of non-Anabaptists who
have voluntarily converted to the Anabaptist way of life; for most congregations, the issue of differentiation has enormous importance. All Anabaptist
groups wrestle with it. For example, the Brethren established a volunteer

service program after World War II. Many young people helped in work with refugees and in repairing the ravages of war (especially in Germany and Austria). Now Mennonites and Brethren continue the same program, partly because it has proven an excellent way for differentiation to occur on the way to adult well-being.

·3·

The Family of God

Sexuality

It is a truism that the Reformation radically altered the perception of sexuality. Some historians say that the Protestant rejection of marriage as a sacrament made marriage more a personal agreement between a man and a woman. Because Protestant marriage was more a matter of agreement than a religious rite, the medieval sense of a woman as sensuous and materialistic disappeared.[1] Whether such a redefinition occurred or not, Protestantism as a whole did not promote equality between men and women. The husband was the head of the family as Christ was the head of the church. In matters of the church, women submitted to male leadership. Yet within the left wing of the Reformation one might expect a step beyond Protestantism. Because of the democratic, congregational nature of Anabaptism, one might expect to see a more evenhanded relation between men and women. Furthermore, the covenantal understanding of community would require a mutual relationship between the sexes. When the individual depends on the community for maturation, a free, mutual interaction between male and female is necessary for the development of self-knowledge and individuation.[2]

So we come to the history of the Anabaptist movement expecting a radical reformation not only in terms of church membership and relationship to the state, but also in the understanding of sexuality. The facts are disappointing. In regard to sexuality one cannot easily distinguish between Anabaptism and the Protestant Reformation. Like Protestants, Anabaptists did not consider marriage a sacrament, and they certainly did not consider women the material source of evil. And like his Protestant counterpart, the Anabaptist husband is head of the house (as Christ is the head of the church), and women are subjected to men. It is not that Anabaptists were more hierarchical than Protestants. What surprises us is that a movement so radical in relation to the dominant church and the state failed to radicalize its own private life — the family.[3]

Despite this disappointment several characteristics of Anabaptist thought on this subject deserve attention. A communal strain runs through the Anabaptist understanding of sexuality. Most notable, of course, was the Münster debacle. Whether Melchior Hofmann (1493–1543) was responsible for Münster will not likely ever be decided. He was convinced that the Second Coming was imminent and that Strasbourg would be the New Jerusalem. Although Hofmann died after ten years in a Strasbourg prison, another Melchiorite, John Matthys, took his apocalyptic convictions to Münster, Germany. Under the leadership of a radical evangelical by the name of Bernard Rothmann, the message caught fire there. In May 1534 the Münsterites formed a New Jerusalem; they affirmed the sharing of goods and the practice of polygamy. In fact, marriage was required, and polygamy became nearly compulsory. On June 25, 1535, Münster fell to the combined forces of Protestant and Catholic bishops.[4] The Münster episode nearly ruined Anabaptism, for the aberrations that occurred there gave opponents the very weapons they needed. Furthermore, it set a course for Anabaptism itself. Just as the persecutions of the sixteenth century caused in Anabaptism those scars that create dissent, so the Münster experiment with polygamy caused scars that led to a rather stern, traditional view of family. Anabaptism never returned to the Münster radicalism. But one cannot practice community of goods and community of purpose without *some* community of family. The Hutterites are prime examples.

Hutterites have always lived in cultures where the family exercises authority over property ownership, child socialization, and mate selection. The Hutterites have insisted on transferring these responsibilities to the community. We have already spoken of their tradition of common property. Leaders also tended to arrange marriages. Hutterites took care that worldly characteristics like love and romantic affection did not interfere with the God-given institution of marriage. Children were handed over to community caretakers soon after birth, though the mother was allowed to nurse the infant. After weaning, the child was nurtured and educated entirely by the community. One Bruderhof (Hutterite) mother writes:

> It is the voluntary decision of each family to give up its children from the first weeks of their life to the education of the community. This is done from the deepest urge and desire that everything in our life may be

communal, and that our little ones may also grow into the community life of the children. We experience in our joyous children that a blessing rests on this: it is not said without reason that education begins during the first days of life.[5]

Husbands and wives worked at different tasks according to sexual groupings, but married couples lived in the same apartment. Put another way, sexual intercourse was a private matter. Even so, birth control has been discouraged by the community.

In contrast, Mennonites and Brethren have stressed the sanctity of the family. Though always under the guidance of divine will and the faith community, decisions regarding property, mate selection, and the socialization of children are a family matter. The community only assists. Sociologist Karl Peter argues that Hutterites may emphasize family independence when their community is under stress. Yet when the community ideology is strong, Hutterites tend to subordinate the family to community even more. By contrast, when the family comes under stress for Mennonites and Brethren, these groups have no choice but to rely on individual piety and responsibility.[6]

The relationship of men to women in Anabaptist communities probably does take on a dimension that differs from the general culture. In the *Martyrs' Mirror* there are some accounts of men and women in prison forming support groups for each other,[7] and this crossing of gender lines suggests a belief that cultural taboos regarding sexuality ought not override the nature of Christian community. It may well be that the primacy of the religious community has indeed overcome the hierarchical structure of the traditional family. If that change has occurred, then the change has appeared only faintly throughout four centuries and only with force in the past decade. Theologically the community "difference" may yet be a potential force in Anabaptism. The first Anabaptists spoke of a spiritual marriage. Later Pietists were influenced by Gottfried Arnold and E. C. Hochmann von Hochenau, who depreciated physical marriage but expressed appreciation for a spiritualized sexuality.[8] While spiritualized marriage could lead to asceticism,[9] it could also transform conventional sexual relationships by placing those relationships in a faith community. Men, who otherwise appropriated for themselves power positions, would enter the faith community as slaves of Jesus Christ. Women, who found acceptance only in subordination to men, would enter the faith community as saints of the new age. In other words, in a "spiritual" community men and women, though still quite different as persons, nevertheless met on the same faith level. While such an understanding of the eschatological community did not at first deeply alter Anabaptism, it may be that eventually Christianity's left wing will indeed become a faith community where men and women are equal partners.

Another theological perception colors the issue of sexuality. Melchior Hofmann believed that Mary's womb was simply the place where the sperm of God, so to speak, developed as Jesus. In other words, contrary to Christian tradition, Jesus was not fully human. Menno Simons extended this view to human conception in general. He believed that fetuses develop from the male's sperm without any contribution from the woman. With such a Christology and such a view of conception it stands to reason that equality of sexes would not be likely to develop quickly among Mennonites.[10]

In the Pietistic roots of the Brethren there was an androgynous Adam who, spiritually, held man and woman in one being. Spiritual marriage was always intended, from the time of Adam, but physical marriage resulted from the Fall. The issue here is critical — so critical it may even be the raison d'être of the Church of the Brethren. A major spiritual "father" of the Brethren, the radical Pietist Gottfried Arnold, held to the spiritual marriage, and his views were shared by many disciples, some of whom influenced the Brethren. In 1701 Arnold disappointed his friends and disciples by marrying Anna Sprögel and taking a professional post in the Lutheran church. Arnold's disciples assumed his marriage to Sprögel was simply spiritual, but a year later the couple's first child was born. Arnold argued, for good reason, that spiritual reality is to be expressed in human life. In 1708 some people in Scharzenau, Germany, heretofore influenced by radical Pietism, followed the new Arnold. They brought the spiritual reality of community into this life. The Church of the Brethren resulted. Brethren eventually rejected radical Pietism's idea of a spiritual marriage and replaced it with a concept of human marriage that exhibited divine qualities (love, forgiveness, and ultimacy). Brethren then expressed an idealism about marriage that differed from the earlier Anabaptist tradition. They believed physical marriage reflected spiritual qualities.

The Mennonite position on gender roles evidently came down to this: women can instruct and nurture children, but they cannot instruct men. This means, in effect, that women cannot preach or teach in the church. One writer put it this way: "Submission is one great secret of home happiness. Lack of subjection brings discord. Woman's place in the church or in the home is one of subjection....Why is there discord in so many Christian homes? Why are saloons filled with men and churches not? Why are boys and girls in tender years drifting into awful sin? Because wives do not take the lowly place God has assigned them."[11] This axiom was first challenged in the twentieth century. For Mennonites the challenge came from an innocent source — the women's sewing circle.[12] Started after World War I, the sewing movement brought women together to create clothing and other articles for foreign missions. Combined with the Sunday school movement, where women had a primary role, these women's groups created opportunities for women to bond with each other and to exercise leadership. As these movements were absorbed into the larger church, women could hardly be denied appropriate leadership roles. The end result of these changing patterns has yet to be realized. But gradually women are taking roles as pastors and teachers. Anabaptist women do not speak as much about change in their personal lives as they do about a redefinition of their role in the faith community. Issues of gender have not yet resulted in a male consciousness movement, and may never do so. But as women redefine their roles in the community of faith, men will likely adjust theirs.[13]

A specific example of the shift in sexual roles can be seen in the matter of dress. Anabaptists have a very strong tendency to maintain the same style of dress as that first worn in Europe.[14] For men it has been button trousers and no ties. Major marks of the Anabaptist woman have been a long dress and a prayer veil (or bonnet in some cases). Whether the veil was a remnant of the original European dress or was worn for the sake of modesty, it has been widely interpreted as a symbol of woman's submission to man (1 Corinthians 11:1–16). At the beginning of this century the veil became a religious marking for Anabaptist groups. In the marketplace, the city, the airport, an Anabaptist woman could be identified by her veil. For many that dress code was satisfying. It gave women a corporate identity in the faith community over against the dominant society. Since about 1950 Mennonite and Brethren women have tended to discard the veil, to reduce its size, or to use appropriate substitutes.[15] Some communities still expect a woman to wear the veil at a religious ceremony, but for the most part the veil as a symbol of female submission has lost its significance. The change of such a meaningful dress code indicates clearly that many women of the Anabaptist tradition are no longer willing to accept a submissive role in gender relationships, and few men ask for it. Men can hardly ask women to wear the veil: they have discarded the broad-brim hat, plain collars, and beards that once identified them as Anabaptists.

With the shift in gender relationships have come a number of problems for Anabaptist communities. Divorce has become more common, for example.[16] Yet many congregations will not call a divorced pastor. Another painful problem is the issue of homosexuality. Everyone has been aware of the presence of homosexuals in the community, but homosexuality itself has received very little attention. As long as homosexual men and women remained in the closet and were not promiscuous, little was said. Relative openness regarding homosexuality in American culture has made possible the development of gay and lesbian groups among Mennonites and Brethren. In 1976 a small group called Brethren/Mennonite Council for Gay Concerns formed to give support to homosexuals and raise consciousness in Mennonite and Brethren circles. The group has grown and has become more open. It publishes its own excellent newsletter and has established its own annual conference. To date no homosexual group has been accepted or recognized by any of the Anabaptist groups. The Brethren/Mennonite Council for Gay Concerns has not yet been allowed publicity or booths at church conferences. Official attempts to deal with homosexuality have been guarded and cautious, to say the least. In 1977 the Church of the Brethren authorized a study of sexuality with specific attention to homosexuality. The committee advocated the primacy of covenant in sexual ethics. That is, the stable covenant of marriage is available to a large number of persons, including homosexuals. The church, in contrast to the committee, however, requires that homosexuals in the church either alter their gender preference or remain celibate. Anabaptists, who live by covenant ethics rather than individualistic rules, are seriously confounded by the presence of gays and lesbians who wish to live in community and develop a family life.[17] It is not certain how community values might eventually encompass these conflicting principles.

The nuclear family lies at the heart of the Anabaptist lifestyle. Anabaptists tend to reject anything that threatens that lifestyle or offers something in its place. While sexual intercourse has not often been limited to reproduction, Anabaptists are deeply aware of the creative nature of human sexuality: men and women were not made simply to enjoy each other but also to generate new life. Although a community ethos can lead to mutual support and friendship between men and women, casual relationships are not acceptable. The left wing of the Reformation may be radical in terms of state, church, and society, but, by necessity, it has been quite conservative in regard to sexuality and family.

Passages

In a close community few things are more important than the celebration of key moments or turning points in an individual's lifetime. The Anabaptist tradition does indeed have a rich tradition for the passages of life, a tradition that bears directly on the health of the community and each individual. Because Anabaptist attitudes toward the passage of life will differ from those of the dominant society, I briefly trace here a lifetime in a communitarian setting.

Children are welcome in the Anabaptist family. There may not be all the trappings of a separate room, a crib, or closets full of toys and clothing, but children are wanted and welcome. Although Anabaptists who have become urbanized would tend to have the same problems that the general population has, there is still a strong tendency to accept a child as a gift of God and as the normal result of family life, an expected member of the community. The practical result of that fundamental assumption has been a reluctance to use birth control. While only the Hutterites officially oppose the use of birth control, the conviction lingers sub rosa in all the groups.[18]

Conception, the beginning of biological life, marks the continuation of the faith community. To stop conception may be equivalent to abortion, for the unborn child has life when it is a known, wanted member of the community. That time cannot be easily determined, but it may even be before conception occurs. Once the fetus has become a member of the community, abortion would be unthinkable. While it would be difficult to state exactly when a fetus becomes a member of the community (when the mother knows it is there?), obviously abortion can hardly ever be the appropriate solution to an unwanted pregnancy.[19]

Family and community celebrate the birth of a child much as other faith communities. Some differences occur early, however. For Anabaptists there is no baptism. The baby has no sin, so there is no need for any salvific act.[20] To be more precise, the baptism of a baby would be considered a gross violation of faith and polity. The baby knows community from the beginning. The baby sits at the table, is held by everyone, and receives constant attention. In a Hutterite community the baby hears prayers, hymns, stories, and Scripture from the beginning. Other Anabaptist communities are not very different. In many communities the child will be dedicated. In the dedicatory service the parents and the faith community are addressed, not the baby. The parents are asked to raise the child in the nurture of the Lord, and the faith community is asked specifically to support the parents and, more or less, act *in loco parentis.* These promises are taken seriously. Anabaptist children learn early that other family members and community members will indeed, on occasion, speak as parents or at least consult with the biological parents about their behavior. There is no place to hide from community (except occasionally behind the barn). In fact, even one's house has an open door. Other children, relatives, and even neighbors may enter unannounced and sometimes without knocking. All these unarticulated signals build in the child a deep sense of community.

The Hutterites are even more programmatic. When children reach the age of three, they are placed in the kindergarten. The child is no longer the family "baby" but one among many peers. While children may have experienced community in the family, in the kindergarten they learn to live in community with others of the same age. They receive loving, attentive care and deliberate instruction. Peter Rideman, a sixteenth-century theological father of the Hutterites, writes that education in community prevents children from carrying out "their headstrong will and carnal practices." They are to be taught divine discipline in a way that public school students are not.[21] Later Hutterites put it more positively:

> In a Church community, where all-embracing love goes into action in the fight against self-will and possessiveness, all childlike qualities can flourish and grow to maturity, developing the powers to work and serve mankind. Here, the children's life is determined by their holy need for faith. Therefore it is guided by the power of faith living in the Church. Here the parents, the educators, and the children themselves are truly functions of the living, all-inclusive unity of the Church. The Church's Spirit of faith and love is the whole that transcends the individual. Its binding, uniting power permits the child to be really a child and in the holy fight saves him from fatal isolation. This power is more than the shared economy of the family; it is more than the limited common interests of blood ties.[22]

At age six the child enters elementary school. No Anabaptist group defies the legal requirements for education, but they do differ in how that requirement is met. Calvin Redekop, a Mennonite historian and sociologist, has identified four types of social organization among Anabaptists, with corresponding educational procedures:[23]

Theocratic: God is sovereign, and religious authority determines every aspect of the common life. The community itself must be quite distinct from the secular world, which is nontheocratic. The theocratic type *must* organize its own schools and utilize its own community members as teachers. The secular society absolutely cannot form the children as community members. Public education will invariably develop the self and will work for self-actualization: the "I" will become more important than the "we." Theocratic education tends to make the "I" and the "we" the same. Hutterites give us a good example of the theocratic model, though now Bruderhof children may attend public schools through high school.

Commonwealth: The community remains sovereign, and geographically definable, but receives permission for such existence from the state. Secular society is therefore recognized, and the church must negotiate with it. The commonwealth society represents the classic Anabaptist two-kingdom system: both church and state exist with divine legitimation. In the commonwealth model the church still develops parochial schools, but they are more like public schools. Children are bused in; teachers are hired according to community standards; state requirements are met. Mennonites, Amish, and some older Brethren groups (especially in Pennsylvania, Ohio, and Indiana) often have this type of parochial school.

Community: Although the church and faith community still exists as a unit and retains authority over the members of the community, it does not exist as a geographical enclave. Members live at various places in the wider community. They work at secular jobs and do business in the general social matrix. For religious meetings they come together at the church. Members of this faith community must depend much more on public education. Young people cannot expect to find their vocation in community tasks; like their parents, they will work and do business entirely in the secular society, so they must learn about that society and its mores. Education for the faith community depends much more on released time, Sunday school, camps, work projects, and family instruction. Apart from the Hutterites, Amish, and some Mennonite communities, most modern-day Anabaptists experience the "community" type of social organization.

Individualistic: Such Anabaptists are much like mainstream Christians. They live completely in the secular society and act as members of that social matrix. For the sake of tradition, or out of an appreciation for Anabaptist values, they attend an Anabaptist church. People in this group are most likely to leave Anabaptists in favor of a more mainstream religious tradition. Their children receive instruction in Anabaptist values through Sunday school or church camp, but they attend public schools.

While their mainline counterparts are preparing for confirmation, the

Anabaptist child is being prepared (passive voice intended) for baptism. In theory baptism marks the transfer from childhood and the old age to adulthood and the new age. Unfortunately baptism often does not match that development in maturation. It may become confused with church membership (and therefore occur earlier), or it may be confused with a conversional second birth and come at the request of the person rather than the congregation.

The shift from childhood to adulthood in Anabaptist communities has been a matter of considerable interest to the psychological and sociological world. For the most part the more communitarian groups (for example, Hutterites) lack the kinds of problems that more secular adolescents face.[24] The pre-adolescent is not fed programs of self-actualization with a large choice of vocations. For the young man only five or ten vocational possibilities exist. For the young woman there are even fewer. Young adults thus have clear expectations about what is possible. The community does not value one vocation above another, and, of course, there cannot be any differential in pay. In traditional Hutterite communities the shift to adulthood, at fourteen or fifteen, entails a considerable change in status. The young persons are now spoken of as *bei die Leut* (with the folk). They eat with the adults rather than the children. They visit other communities as adults (though not for weddings and funerals until after they have been baptized). They receive the same privileges (including a private allowance and personal supply of alcoholic beverages) that other adults do.

Young men are assigned tasks on the labor force. They receive a saw, a hammer, a pitchfork, and a spade. Young women, who have fewer vocational possibilities, are assigned a task and are given paint brushes, kitchen knives, a broom, a hoe, and knitting needles. Young men are given a small chest for their private possessions, while young women are given a medium-size chest. Both are given clothing or cloth for adult dress.[25] Sometime after this shift to adult status — around age nineteen for young women and somewhat later for young men — Hutterite youth will move toward baptism.

Hutterites understand that the maturation process can be disruptive. Some breaking of the mores can be expected. Most of the violations are minor, yet they are conscious forays beyond the boundary. Research psychologist Joseph Eaton lists as common "sins" the writing of secret letters and notes, masturbation, reading racy magazines, necking, telling dirty stories, and posing for pictures.[26] These are minor transgressions, and the Anabaptist tradition does not exaggerate their importance. Adults tend to define sin in such a way that young people do not easily develop a deep sense of guilt.

For Anabaptists, children are born good. Ill behavior cannot be defined as sin. To be a sin, an offense must be done willfully and knowingly. Anabaptists assume that children cannot independently act willfully and knowingly, so children can hardly sin. One of my own potent memories goes back to age twelve at Camp Mack, near Fort Wayne, Indiana. Somehow a child evangelist slipped into the camp program. At the Friday evening campfire the evangelist tried to convict us of sin and offer the grace of God. We were asked to write on a piece of paper our major sin and throw it in the fire. Later several of us boys asked as many young people as possible what sin they had thrown into the fire. Everyone had thrown in a blank piece of paper! Sin does not come easily until the Anabaptist youth reaches the age of accountability.

The Hutterite system of formation may be more radically consistent, but it points to characteristics that are reflected throughout Anabaptism. From an early age children are taught to live in community. Privacy is not held in high esteem; indeed, too much of a sense of privacy may be considered a sign of alienation. Sunday schools, parochial schools, camps, and colleges stress process as much as information and knowledge. Children are considered good, and sin is not recognized until there is some notion of adult accountability.

As young people pass from adolescence to adulthood, they may, even should, experience freedom to test the community and its lifestyle. Presumably the *felix culpa* (blessed fall) occurs at about age sixteen. Baptism marks the shift from childhood to the adult community. Nevertheless, baptism in the Anabaptist tradition does presuppose a change of life; it does not simply mark a graduation from one stage to the next. The young person is asked to renounce Satan, to forgo the evil ways of the world, and to accept Jesus Christ as Lord. Implicit is a shift from the old age to the new age. Baptism is not a conversion in the sense of repentance, but a conscious recognition that the old is gone and that one now enters the community of the new age.

For the baptized young adult, participation in the faith community is a given. Only in the "individualistic" type of social organization can one make a choice regarding participation. To be in the community of the new age means that one's identity meshes with the faith community. The adult participates, accepts assignments, and finds in the church the central structure of life. Absences are noticed and often must be explained. In some cases the group will not meet if someone is absent or if there is an unexplained absence (because an absence alters the nature of the community, even explained absences can stop the meeting).

After baptism the young Anabaptist adult moves toward marriage. Marriage within the faith community may be the most important step he or she ever takes. In Hutterite communities it is a joyful two-day celebration. In less intentional or close communities the marriage has not lost its happy significance, but the ritual may be limited to a ceremony, reception, and communal meal. Marriage itself, for the most part, is considered a given. In the population over fourteen years of age the number of unmarried among Mennonites (especially males) is significantly lower than among the general population. At the same time, of course, the number of married but not separated would be much higher (10–15 percent more). In contrast to society at large, Anabaptist society has almost no divorced or married but separated persons. Even widows and widowers are significantly fewer. Despite the obvious stability of Anabaptist families, one cannot say they are built on romantic love. Marriage has a serious communitarian quality — it is a union that enhances community life. Peter Rideman, a sixteenth-century Hutterite, wrote of marriage in a theocratic community:

> Marriage is a union of two, in which one taketh the other to care for and the second submitteth to obey the first, and thus through their agreement two become one, and are no longer two but one. But if this to be done in a godly way they must come together not through their own action and choice, but in accordance with God's will and order, and therefore neither leave nor forsake the other but suffer both ill and good together all their days.[27]

No one would care to say that love does not exist among Anabaptist couples, but certainly marriages are not dependent simply on the sometimes fickle nature of romantic love. Marriage carries with it a bonding that is also rooted in the bonding of the faith community. Any decision to separate or divorce involves also the wider bonding.

Life's final passage, death, may be perceived differently in a communitarian setting than it is from an individualistic perspective. The individualist hopes for some type of personal immortality in which the "soul" continues to possess individual traits like enjoyment, recognition of others, reunion with friends, and pleasant pastimes. The communitarian hopes for restoration to the community through a new, refined mode of existence. If the individualist did expect a resurrection of the body, it would probably be a rather literal resuscitation of his or her physical body. A communitarian expects to participate in a new way with the present corporate body. Just as the beginning of life can be identified with the fetus's link to the mother and, through her, the community, death occurs for the communitarian when isolation has occurred — that is, when the person can no longer interact with the community. And like birth, death cannot be defined simply biologically. As we shall see below, Anabaptists tend to keep the dying at home. Present-day Anabaptists, like many others, support the hospice movement as a means of keeping the community intact while one of its members is dying. Because community death can occur before biological death, Anabaptists tend to avoid heroic measures, especially over a long period. Sustaining a true relationship with the dying is more important than prolonging a life for a few more days. Mennonite and Brethren health groups advocate living wills and formal instructions regarding life-support measures. At the same time, the taking of biological life before community death occurs creates serious problems for the person's continued (resurrected) life with the community. Consequently, suicide and euthanasia have no real place in life's final moments.

Morality

The meaning of life passages largely determines the moral issues of health care delivery. Anabaptists start with the premise that life decisions are based on community good (not necessarily "common good") rather than individual survival or justice. Some of the moral conclusions drawn from this premise may be startling to the noncommunitarian observer, but they are normally congruent with the primary presupposition. It is the definition of life itself that makes the differences.

As we have seen in the discussion about passages, life is not to be defined strictly biologically. Life is measured by the quality of satisfaction realized in one's own community. Life is created by formation within community, and satisfactory life requires an acceptable level of group participation. Otherwise illness in some form will occur. As in any shame/honor system satisfaction in life depends more on being an integral member of the community than on maintaining biological existence. Anabaptists "normally" recognize that they are products of their continuing formation and do not presume to have an existence independent of what has been given to them by that formation (even if they leave it).

We could start a discussion of morality anywhere in life's process, but let us begin with birth. The fertilization of an egg is not the beginning of life. Life begins when the fetus becomes a part of the community. This distinction resembles the difference made between *vitality* (biological) and *humanity* (developmental).[28] "Becoming part of the community" is difficult to define, but when the mother, at least, is aware of the existence of a new child, then life has begun.[29] One might suppose that abortion would be acceptable before that sense of awareness occurs — as indeed it might, especially in the case of an unwanted child or a defective fetus — but, for the most part, the sense of belonging comes so quickly that abortion is nearly impossible.[30] Nevertheless, although abortion is nearly unthinkable in the Anabaptist context, a community separated from the state would not insist that its ethic become national policy. Consequently, Anabaptists are in fact "pro-life" within the faith community, but because of their refusal to dictate public morality, they appear to be "pro-choice" in the national debate. For example, the first national statement of the Church of the Brethren on abortion was gladly used by pro-choice forces. When eventually it became clear that the Church of the Brethren would be identified nationally as a pro-choice group, the church membership at its annual conference altered the statement to make protection of the fetus clear.[31]

One cannot predict exactly when the new child will become a member of the community. Certainly it is possible so to anticipate the birth of a child that it can become a member even before conception. Anabaptist couples expect (and are expected by others) to have children as a natural part of life; as a result, most Anabaptists do not countenance the continued prevention of conception.[32] From a community perspective the prevention of conception may seem like abortion. A new child belongs to the community. An Anabaptist couple does not have the "individualistic" right to deprive the community of a child.[33] That is, birth control may enable a couple to regulate the size of their family and allow them to enjoy sex for its own sake, but, from the community perspective, the continued use of contraceptives thwarts a primary function of the sexual act. The sexual act is not to be understood as strictly and merely a matter of procreation — companionship and pleasure are other gifts from human sexuality — so continence after marriage as a means of birth control is practically unknown (though the story is told that Calvin married an Anabaptist woman so he would not be disturbed in his studies).

Of course there can be more than one interpretation concerning the moral aspects of a lifestyle. That is particularly true here. Most demographers assume that Anabaptists eschew birth control because the community grows primarily through reproduction rather than conversion.[34] And indeed Anabaptists generally do have large families. For example, the Amish have an average of seven children per family, and Hutterite families eight.[35] But few religious groups make such basic decisions solely on the basis of economic or demographic advantage. New life is a divine gift to the community.

It is well known that persons who are dying gradually isolate themselves from society and family.[36] In communitarian societies such isolation is not just a precursor of death — it is a form of death itself. Seen in this light the preservation of biological life as such has little value. Indeed, it could be considered morally wrong to save a biological life that has already become isolated. Consequently, heroic measures to save life are not as desirable as they might be to noncommunitarians.[37]

Likewise no one has the right to isolate a person or remove from the community one who still participates in the life of the community. Extended periods of hospitalization may be morally wrong for the Anabaptist patient; the attempt to prolong biological life may prematurely end one's life in the community. Similarly, Anabaptists look askance at any use of technology or drugs that might impair the community relationship. Intensive care units create physical isolation; drugs that cause altered states of mind create psychological isolation. And it would be morally wrong to end biological life by suicide or euthanasia *before* participation in the community had ended — the individual must be allowed to reach the point of death as a community member.

All modern Anabaptists have been influenced to some extent by the Prohibition movement, so in most though not all groups tobacco and alcohol tend to be restricted, sometimes even strictly forbidden.[38] In recent years tobacco and alcohol have been seen as narcotics that both alter the personality and create a health hazard. Anabaptists oppose the use of chemical substances to alter personality or increase social volubility — they assume that meaningful social contact derives from the faith interaction. Not only are chemical substances unnecessary; they impair true interaction. In fact, at a deeper level it is assumed that the social network will control and define personality adjustment, so chemical assistance is not necessary.[39] The individual who seems to lack acceptance or peer relationships will indeed find it in the faith community — unless a chemical substance is used that clouds the process. Or put another way, it is the lack of group support that leads to the use of substances.

Without being dogmatic Anabaptists also tend to shy away from the use of mind-altering drugs to create social adjustment. Should phenothiazine be used to treat schizophrenia or at least to keep the patient acceptably tranquil? Anabaptists assume that schizophrenia is a problem of social formation that should be addressed in terms of the patient's social environment. Or should children be given depressants in order to assist them in the classroom? While Anabaptists would wish every child to have a useful educational experience, they would say that the child's environment should be readjusted rather than the child's psyche altered by means of chemical substances.

It should be abundantly clear that Anabaptist ethics depend on the function of the person in the community. An ontological or absolute ethic would be difficult to find in this tradition. Consequently, Anabaptists must consider carefully every decision.[40] Such decision making reflects the nature of Anabaptist morality.

A morality based on the function of the person in the community works well for close-knit groups, but applying that same ethic to national policy presents a much more difficult problem. Anabaptists tend to believe in the goodness of creation and the covenantal nature of all humanity. They generally assume that people will act for the preservation of their human community and will act in a caring way for all others. The Anabaptist does not think first of an immoral society. Consequently, in the public arena, the Anabaptist ethic tends to appear naive and too trusting of human compassion.

A number of current issues illustrate the moral dilemma for Anabaptists. Take, for example, the use of fetal tissue for the treatment of such an illness as Parkinson's disease. At first glance there would appear to be no problem with the use of fetal tissue: fetal tissue made available following a miscarriage could be thought of in the same way as the organs of a deceased person. Anabaptists would rejoice that recently developed medical techniques make it possible for damaged persons once again to participate in the human community. But the possibility of abuse is enormous. Children could be conceived as a resource for fetal tissue; mothers could be encouraged to abort in order to "help" someone else. Anabaptists could not countenance the abuse of one person in order to bring healing to another. Anabaptists do believe that congregational health support groups and hospital ethics committees have a role to play in decision making on this issue, but until such groups become legally empowered to make decisions with and for those unable to speak for themselves, Anabaptists will likely oppose the use of fetal tissue as an accepted practice.

The same thinking applies to genetic engineering. The use of genetic engineering in agriculture offers incredible possibilities for increasing the world's food resources, allowing crops like maize to be grown in environments that lack water and rich topsoil. Anabaptists, who come largely from rural areas, can appreciate the purposes of genetically engineering plants, and they understand the world's need for improved food resources. Indeed, Anabaptists are directly involved in the development of new varieties of plants and animals that are hardier and more productive.[41]

In addition, Anabaptists applaud the use of genetic engineering to produce such lifesaving pharmaceuticals as insulin or interferon. But again Anabaptists have deep fears about interfering with the genetics of the human community. Despite their high level of concern for persons throughout the world, Anabaptists would say that stable community cannot be developed by genetically designing a model person. The potential for such a use forces Anabaptists to be very reluctant to support large-scale genetic experimentation.

·4·

One and the Many

Dignity

For the Anabaptist there are three aspects of dignity. They all inter-twine in such a way that it becomes difficult to separate them, yet, because each belongs to such a different realm of discourse, it will be best to take them one at a time. They are (1) the sense of honor in the community, (2) humility (*Gelassenheit* — the surrender of will and personal ambition to God), and (3) the practice of living a simple life.

Honor

As I indicated above, the Anabaptist society is based on a system of honor and shame rather than law and guilt. In a law-oriented society the individual is expected to live according to the regulations of the social ma-trix, and this law-abiding behavior is presumed to bring satisfaction in life. Those who cannot or do not live according to regulations bring a sense of guilt upon themselves. The guilt derives from a sense of imperfection or from the willful desire for self-satisfaction. Needless to say, some societies can develop such a strong sense of law that certain individuals suffer from considerable guilt.[1] Other societies have such a low sense of law that little guilt falls on the individual.

In a law-guilt system the youth becomes an adult by means of a *felix culpa*, or blessed fall. Young people will never be adults unless as conscious individuals they do that which they know to be sin. Following the fall, in-dividuals will continue to experience guilt and forgiveness, but at the same time they will be able to make adult decisions. They do not simply follow regulations but know the consequences of their actions. In that sense they

51

have become adults. And, in the law-guilt system, there is no other way to become an adult. In the law-guilt system each person has a conscience formed by either divine revelation or the social matrix. In the conscience, then, the individual has a trustworthy guide for living according to the law of his or her culture.

In an honor-shame system the child has been formed by the intimate community (family, tribe, faith community). The child learns early that satisfaction in life comes from acceptance by the community and conformance to its standards. Failure to conform with the standards causes a loss of acceptance and therefore a sense of shame. The sense of shame can be felt by the child at an early age (guilt probably comes later). In an honor-shame system the child becomes an adult by testing the system ("leaving home"). Away from home (either figuratively or actually) young people may (or may not) learn that honor comes within the community that formed them. At that point the young person can make a choice, and with the making of a choice the youth becomes an adult. Conscience, having been formed by the faith community, can be trusted to tell the members when they are out of step.

For the Anabaptist, dignity lies in the adult decision to accept and live in honor in the faith community. Such dignity does not depend on financial success, institutional position, or academic level. Dignity is available to anyone regardless of position and success. Everyone has a place. Despite the hierarchical nature of the Anabaptist family there is also a clear dignity for women. If a woman chooses the honor-shame system of the family and community, she has considerable honor as wife, mother, community participant, educator, counselor, and confidant. Her role is not the same as a man's, but her honor is the same, and her dignity derives from that sense of community honor.

One can sometimes tell the character of an ethos by how people try to escape it. When people raised in a law-guilt system attempt to break the pattern, they normally relativize the law or even become antinomian (opposed to laws). When people raised in an honor-shame system try to break the pattern, they become individualists. Anabaptists, who may be inherently anarchical anyway,[2] seldom become antinomian. Nonetheless, sociological literature written by Mennonites and Brethren is replete with warnings that Anabaptists are becoming hopelessly individualistic.

Humility

Humility is a necessary ingredient of community life. When persons raise self above community, community becomes impossible. The apostle Paul thought there must be pride somewhere among the quarreling Corinthian Christians — otherwise how would they know they even had "pillar" members (1 Corinthians 11:18–19; 4:6–7)? In a close community individuation (awareness of one's unique characteristics and contribution) would normally be a desirable characteristic, but individualism (placing self over against community) will destroy the sense of community. All Anabaptist groups emphasize the importance of humility. Mennonites speak of it as *Gelassenheit,* which could be translated as humility but might better be translated as self-denial, mutuality, or participation in community consensus.[3] Mennonite sociologist Calvin Redekop describes it as "forcing the submission of the *rational* will (reason) to the will of Christ; submitting the *human will* of self-advancement to the will of Christ; denying human lusts and passions by transforming them to serve others; and dedicating life to the service of the Kingdom of God in the community and beyond."[4] Since *Gelassenheit* makes the Anabaptist community possible, in no way is it to be understood as low self-esteem or lack of dignity. To the contrary, a strong sense of mutuality gives dignity to the Anabaptist, where success, wealth, position, or education would have failed.

Much of the piety of the Anabaptist tradition stresses this quality of humility. Jesus exhibited such self-giving, and we will be happy in community if we do likewise. An early hymn stresses the function of humility:

> How *pleasant* is it and how *good*
> That those who live as brothers should
>   In faith and love uniting,
> Like servants wash each other's feet
> When at the feast of love they meet,
>   In fellowship *delighting.*
>
> 'Tis precious and of *honored* worth.
> Our Lord himself, while here on earth,
>   His deep love demonstrating,
> In true humility of heart
> Stooped down to play the servant's part,
>   This practice consecrating.

The hymn does not stress humility as a virtue. The mutual attitude allows one to know his or her vocation in the faith community:

> Who spurns the washing of his feet[5]
> Thus spurns a fellowship replete,
>   No vital touch sustaining.
> His life in Jesus cannot start;
> His selfish soul must *stand apart,*
> A *withered vine remaining.*
>
> Within Thy vineyard, Lord, we pray
> Make us green, fruitful vines today,
>   *To each his part assigning.*
> Fill us with love and peace this hour;
> Endow us with Thy Spirit's power,
>   Our hearts to Thee inclining.[6]

Dignity, in a strange way, perhaps, lies in humility within the community. I heard a story recently that illustrates my point here. An anthropologist wished to develop an artistic account of a primitive South American tribe. In order to set up the panoramas he needed plaster casts of some tribe members. One young woman was chosen for a plaster cast. She was absolutely mortified. In order to have the cast made she had to come forward and be identified. Such uniqueness became shame. The Anabaptist sense of shame and honor works in the same way. To be treated differently causes shame.

Church discipline in the Anabaptist tradition normally includes some distancing of the sanctioned person from the community. "Banning" or "avoidance" meant the person was not allowed to attend the corporate functions of the congregation. It could also imply or require a suspension of communication with congregational members and even one's family. Such action intends to shame the person so disciplined in such a way that behavior or attitude modification will occur. Banning not only separates the member from family and community but also makes the disciplined member different from the others. He or she is shamed simply by such individual attention.

The pain of a guilty conscience or fear of punishment furnishes social control in the law-guilt system. The pain of shame furnishes social control in the honor-shame system. In the law-guilt system some compensation must be paid for the transgression. From such a background comes our forensic sense of justification (the blood of Christ was shed for our sins). In the honor-shame system restoration to the community occurs by reconciliation. In most Anabaptist communities this can be accomplished with less difficulty than might be expected. Normally the person under discipline can make a confession before the congregation or elders. Reacceptance is nearly spontaneous and complete. Almost every congregation has at least one story of a young man who strayed, confessed, and was fully restored. Shame can be overcome by expressing appropriate humility before the congregation.

The Simple Life

For the "plain people" of American history few practices could be more important than that of the simple life. All Anabaptists share it. Next to peacemaking it may be the most significant mark of the Anabaptist world.

Of course, like all basic practices, the simple life is rooted in the New Testament. The words of Jesus in the Sermon on the Mount are determinative:

> "Therefore I tell you, do not worry about your life, what you will eat or what you will drink, or about your body, what you will wear. Is not life more than food, and the body more than clothing? Look at the birds of the air; they neither sow nor reap nor gather into barns, and yet your heavenly Father feeds them. Are you not of more value than they? And can any of you by worrying add a single hour to your span of life? And why do you worry about clothing? Consider the lilies of the field, how they grow; they neither toil nor spin, yet I tell you, even Solomon in all his glory was not clothed like one of these. But if God so clothes the grass of the field, which is alive today and tomorrow is thrown into the oven, will he not much more clothe you—you of little faith? Therefore do not worry, saying, 'What will we eat?' or 'What will we drink?' or 'What will we wear?' For it is the Gentiles who strive for all these things; and indeed your heavenly Father knows that you need all these things. But strive first for the kingdom of God and his righteousness, and all these things will be given to you as well. So do not worry about tomorrow, for tomorrow will bring worries of its own. Today's trouble is enough for today." (Matthew 6:25–34)[7]

Few Anabaptists would quarrel with this text. Jesus taught that anxiety for material things would be destructive to a faithful life. And there lies deep in the Anabaptist soul the conviction that God will provide what is needed (and when you do not need much, that makes faith even more simple).

But despite the power of Jesus' words about simple living, the conviction did not really start here. Anabaptists have depended more on texts like Romans 12:1–2:

> I appeal to you therefore, brothers and sisters, by the mercies of God, to present your bodies as a living sacrifice, holy and acceptable to God, which is your spiritual worship. *Do not be conformed to this world,* but be transformed by the renewing of your minds, so that you may discern what is the will of God — what is good and acceptable and perfect. (emphasis added)

Early Anabaptists rejected the excesses of the world at large and expressed the clear intention to live a simple life with few if any luxuries, a simple way of dressing, and a lifestyle that did not depend on developing technology and industrialism. Most Anabaptists still do not own expensive houses, luxurious automobiles, perfumes, and fancy furniture. For decades clothing was kept simple, much like the Swiss, German, or Dutch dress from which it derived. To this day many cannot shift to conventional modern clothing. Many Anabaptists will not purchase or utilize recent technological advances. Some have no electricity, and many have no radios or television. In Pennsylvania, Ohio, Indiana, Missouri, or Kansas one may still encounter buggies driven by people in plain clothes (usually Amish). The Amish represent Anabaptism in a particular form of cultural rejection, but the instinct lies in all the branches. There is a dignity that derives from living (preserving) a particular lifestyle and holding to important traditions — most of which set one apart from society as a whole.

Anabaptist writers use the sociological distinction between *Gemeinschaft* and *Gesellschaft* to explore this separate standing within the larger culture. *Gemeinschaft* refers to the small community which lives out of mutual trust, common beliefs, and generally accepted goals and values. *Gesellschaft* refers to society in general which, in contrast to the communal nature of the *Gemeinde*, depends on capitalism and self-initiative. Its ties are educational and professional rather than religious and familial.[8] Anabaptists look to the past as an ideal time of *Gemeinschaft.* They fear present trends toward *Gesellschaft.* Amish and Hutterites try to avoid the problem by disassociating themselves from society at large. Mennonites and Brethren are fair game for the capitalistic spirit. A colony of agriculturally based Anabaptists can, and usually does, grow at a remarkable rate; the resulting affluence may cause the faith *Gemeinde* to shift to an economic *Gesellschaft.* Redekop describes it as the shift from *meetinghouse* to *countinghouse.*[9]

Probably paucity of possessions goes hand in hand with nonconformity, yet simplicity stands for more than mere dissent. There is a theological concern in living the simple economic life. Practicing the simple life does not imply ipso facto a rejection of culture. It has to do with the suspicion that materialism stands as antithetical to faith. Such a concern has been with Anabaptists from the beginning. Certainly early Hutterites believed that community of goods would bypass the individual's desire to possess things, or even to amass more possessions than needed (wealth or ostentation). The sixteenth-century Hutterite Peter Rideman made clear the theological import of this rejection of materialism:

> Now, he who thus becometh free from created things can then grasp what is true and divine; and when he graspeth it and it becometh his treasure, he turneth his heart towards it, emptieth himself of all else and taketh naught as his, and regardeth it no longer as his but as of all God's children. Therefore we say that as all the saints have community in spiritual gifts, still much more should they show this in material things, and not ascribe the same to and covet them for themselves, for they are not their own; but regard them as of all God's children, that they may thereby show that they are partakers in the community of Christ and are renewed into God's likeness. For the more man yet cleaveth to created things, appropriateth and ascribeth such to himself, the further doth he show himself to be from the likeness of God and the community of Christ.[10]

While Hutterite communities cannot extricate themselves from the economic life of their particular social matrix, individuals living in such communities do not experience the materialism that often marks society at large.

Not all Anabaptists have practiced community of goods, of course. For most the simple lifestyle was a mark of nonconformity. But somewhere at the end of the nineteenth century or the beginning of the twentieth, Anabaptists begin to speak of the simple life rather than nonconformity. For Brethren the issue of ties, hats, veils, and carpets had run its course. In 1908 a Brethren elder, H. C. Early, wrote, "In opposition to parading the empty, carnal life of the worldly throng whose only aim is to make a 'fair show' before men, the strongest plea is made to live the simple life exemplified by Jesus and taught by the apostles."[11]

Those who practice the simple life do not reject the cultural practices of the social matrix — they simply grant them no final value.[12] When the materials and achievements of this world have lost their value, the person can be free.[13] Dignity derives from that sense of freedom from materialism, from any ultimate values attached to the culture.

Community of goods has been the most consistent approach to the simple life. And voices within Anabaptism continue to call for the communal ownership found in a base, or intentional, community.[14] But, by and large, Mennonites and Brethren have adopted an economic stance that Mennonite sociologists have called the "radical confrontation" model. It is a "non-resistant approach to economic life."[15] Essentially the individual can own property but should use possessions to counteract the economic policies of society. The following standards have been suggested:

1. Private property is not rejected, but materialism is.

2. Individual believers will be ready to help their neighbors with financial and material resources as well as services (mutual aid).

3. Individual believers are committed to the concept of stewardship of all resources and possessions. They are responsible for material as well as nonmaterial resources and may not use them detrimentally for their enhancement.

4. Individual believers avoid economic practices that undermine the ethic of the kingdom of God (the human community).[16]

This description of radical confrontation matches in most respects the concept of the simple life. Anabaptist sociologists tend to claim that the simple life and protest economics are no longer operative in Anabaptist circles. It is difficult to argue with statistics, but generally speaking it seems to me that Anabaptist economics are still alive. Sociologists J. Howard Kauffman and Leland Harder note that about 80 percent of Mennonites still believe in mutual aid, and over 50 percent believe there should be Mennonite programs of mutual aid.[17] Brethren still have a sense of the simple life. More than 90 percent say they take into consideration the church's teaching on simple life when they purchase clothing. And nearly 50 percent criticize the materialism of U.S. society.[18] Anyone who attends an Anabaptist conference or mingles with Anabaptists at ecumenical conferences can quickly recognize a difference in dress, combustibles, and entertainments. One may argue that such a lifestyle stems from a pecuniary motivation, but, wealthy or not, most of us who are called Anabaptists still feel called to the simple life. It carries with it the dignity of imperturbability.

Madness

Though mental health has been a major concern of many Anabaptists in this century, it is difficult to find any clear definition of either madness or even mental health itself. One reason for the lack of definition is the reluctance for an Anabaptist to accept popular definitions of good mental health. Anabaptists can hardly use the criterion of social acceptance, for example, when they themselves do not seek general social acceptance as a value for the religious community. Elmer Ediger, director of a Mennonite mental health center, has written a short history of mental illness, which probably illustrates, by default, the Anabaptist attitude toward madness.[19] Ediger accepts Michel Foucault's thesis that society needs madness.[20] Sometimes mad people are scapegoats, while at other times they have represented the supernatural world — perhaps the dark world of the evil spirits, or fools, or, in the sixteenth century, those who could utter "truths" not speakable by responsible citizens. According to Ediger, mad people came on evil times during the age of reason. The loss of the supernatural connection made mad people a danger to reasonable society. Consequently they were placed in despicable institutions. Treatment might include burning blisters on a shaved head in order to draw out the madness. Other treatments might be bleeding induced by leeches or razor blades; chemicals to cause vomiting or diarrhea; hot and cold showers; or even a primitive shock treatment.

The first attempts to break from this disgraceful practice came from the peace churches (probably because the peace churches held to the inherent goodness of the individual person, and Quakers even believed there was a divine spark in each person). British Quakers were alarmed by the death of a Quaker woman in the York (England) Asylum. In 1792 a certain William Tuke urged the Quakers to start their own institution. Four years later, at the newly established York Retreat, "restraint and abuse were replaced by kindness and tolerance, by working in the garden and gentle exercise on the surrounding grounds, by light recreations and amusements."[21]

In 1817 a Friends Asylum was opened in Philadelphia. The treatment there followed the practices at York. The "moral treatment" followed three principles: (1) no one is completely insane; (2) the mentally ill are to be treated in a community context; (3) unacceptable behavior will be treated by the shame of isolation until the behavior stops.[22]

The other peace churches (Mennonites and Brethren) were interested in the mental health problem, but they did not create any hospitals or clinics at that time, even though other groups did follow the Quaker lead.

When finally at the beginning of the twentieth century Anabaptists did start to develop institutions for the mentally ill, they followed the pattern of such famous institutions as Gheel in Belgium or Bethel bei Bielefeld in Germany. At Gheel it was thought that Saint Dympna, patron saint for the mentally ill, had the power to cure madness. Many made a pilgrimage to the shrine. But more important, the community people of Gheel opened their homes to the pilgrims as they awaited the cure. Even today the community offers home care rather than strictly hospital care. Bethel bei Bielefeld, founded by Lutherans in the Pietist healing tradition, was established to provide care for epileptics in a community setting. Since its beginning it has grown to be a very large "town" with schools, job training, work opportunities, shopping centers, and clinics for several types of mentally ill and disabled persons. The first Anabaptist psychiatric hospital, Bethania, was built in Russia in 1910. A second hospital, Bethesda, was started in 1932 at Vineland, Ontario, with awareness of such precedents as York, Gheel, and Bethel. One visitor to Bethesda reported, "The whole spirit of this hospital is in the tradition of a genuine, warm Christian family in contrast to the harshness of a huge state mental institution. The patients carry on quite a normal life, not living under lock and key, daily working on the farm, eating and worshiping together."[23]

The real impetus for engaging in mental health work came from the experiences of conscientious objectors during World War II. The U.S. Selective Training and Service Act of 1940 provided an alternative to military service for conscientious objectors. The program was known as Civilian Public Service or, more popularly, CPS. The conscientious objectors and peace church leaders wanted to establish programs of relief and reconciliation overseas, but some members of the government were reluctant to let other countries know about the pacifist movement in America. Eventually a program was developed for alternative service in psychiatric hospitals throughout the United States. The conscientious objectors, representing many denominations but primarily Brethren, Mennonites, Methodists, and Quakers, were assigned to hospital units established by the peace churches.

The procedure was not always a happy one. Rural Brethren and Mennonites did not at first fit well into the routine of hospitals of any kind. Furthermore, the conscientious objectors were often stunned by the conditions they found in the hospitals. The conscientious objectors complained, often loudly enough to be heard by the media (see, for example, *Life* magazine, May 6, 1946), about the inhumane conditions found in mental institutions. The complaints, expressed with political naiveté, caused hostility and turmoil within some hospitals. But eventually the complaints resulted in action. In 1946 the CPS men formed an organization called the National Mental Health Foundation (NMHF). Despite their original involvement in the formation of the NMHF, the Mennonites eventually founded their own mental health organization, the Mennonite Mental Health Services (MMHS). Quakers and Brethren agreed to cooperate with the Mennonites in their enterprise but chose to support the NMHF and so influence public policies.[24]

The Brethren did continue their involvement with mental health, but it was the Mennonites who did the remarkable. Since 1947 the MMHS has overseen the building of eight mental health clinics throughout North America. The first clinic, the Brook Lane Psychiatric Center, near Leitersburg, Maryland, was authorized by the Mennonites in 1947, and its first patients were admitted in 1949. Shortly afterward Kings View Homes, near Reedley, California, and Philhaven, near Lebanon, Pennsylvania, also began operation. With eight clinics now completed, the Mennonites operate one-fourth of all Protestant mental health facilities. All take an approach to mental health that treats the individual as a member of his or her community, both in the clinic and in the community of the patient's origin.

The Anabaptist commitment to the mental health movement deserves considerable reflection. Of course, deep in the heart of Anabaptists lies the conviction that community creates good mental health for individuals, while individualism causes personal breakdown. The community shares the burdens (and joys) of family, economics, social structures, vocation, and faith. The individual member of a community can live an entire life virtually free of the personal crises caused by these major facets of life and the decisions they entail. Because of such community support for the individual, Anabaptists, especially the Hutterites, have been a favorite object for psychological research.[25] Research demonstrates a remarkable stability within the Anabaptist society; for example, one study notes that

> in the history of the [Hutterite] sect since their coming into the United States [North America?], only one suicide, one divorce and two separations have occurred. There is no known case of parental abandonment of children and no incidence of arson, personal violence, or attempted homicide. No sex crimes are known to have occurred although the Hutterites disclose knowledge of a few instances where their own strict sex mores have been violated during the present generation. These instances, to any reader of the Kinsey report, would hardly warrant the lifting of an eyebrow![26]

The data suggest that Hutterites are half as likely as other homogenous ethnic groups to develop mental illness. And in light of the way Hutterites deal with mental disorder it is noteworthy that recidivism is only half that of those treated in other populations. Joseph Eaton divides Hutterite therapeutic practices into secular and religious practices: secular remedies include family nursing care, protection from social-psychological stress, occupational therapy, some amateur chiropractic, receiving visitors from other colonies, and travel to other colonies; religious activities that promote healing include community prayer and communal confession, within the context of a salvific community. Recidivism is light because the community so quickly accepts and forgets.

Eaton believes the Hutterite community deals best with manic-depressive types, who respond to consistent support, but has more difficulty with schizophrenics, who cannot fully accept the community value system. He also believes the powerful Hutterite process of social-ization can reestablish very well the person with psychic problems, but it does so by fitting the individual into a cultural straitjacket. In contrast, modern psychotherapy encourages clients to make a personal modification of their culture. Hutterite "psychiatry" orients the person toward the future (eschatology) with the advice to dispense with the past and damaging introspection. Modern psychotherapists believe persons will be free when they can accept the vagaries of their formative past.

Needless to say, a sense of the importance of community wholeness has deeply influenced all branches of Anabaptism. The contribution of Anabaptist mental health clinics and community health programs has been enormous, and undoubtedly will contribute worldwide to a revolution in medical delivery. But there are some cautions. First, can Anabaptists, perhaps Mennonites in particular, actually come to some rapprochement with psychology? The answer is not obvious. Anabaptists in general, and Mennonites in particular, have expended much of their intellectual and faith energy in the matter of mental health. Have Anabaptists been diverted from other issues that might better strengthen the faith community? Or worse yet, has psychology invaded the Anabaptist ethos in such a way that the sense of community has become endangered? Sociologist Calvin Redekop claims that psychology is the worst thing that has happened to the Mennonites.[27] A survey of psychological literature written by Anabaptists does leave one with the feeling that, through psychology, individualism can erode the Anabaptist sense of community.[28]

There is yet another problem. The strong Anabaptist community can encourage the individual to "repress" the past. Just where is the Anabaptist dark side? Are Anabaptists devoid of a dark side? Has it been repressed into the forgettable past? Can there be creativity without a "vibrant" dark side? Or are Anabaptists trapped in a lifestyle which demonstrates a stodgy (and useful) determination with little capability of creative flexibility for the twenty-first century?

We have noted already one major reason for the Anabaptist interest and success with mental health programs: like those who show symptoms of "madness" the Anabaptists themselves do not march to the same drum as the dominant culture. In a sense Anabaptists are the very insane of whom Foucault spoke. Anabaptists have reflected very little on the nature of their own dark side. Does the fascination of Anabaptism for the insane of our culture actually point to its own communal dark side? When Anabaptists *must* always stand over against culture, have they expressed their own dark side? Anabaptist dress, language, lifestyle, and attitudes reflect a consistent opposition to the majority. There may be no reason for this lifestyle other than to stand apart. Is this the dark side that keeps Anabaptism alive and even cohesive? With a bit of whimsy I will narrate an incident from our home:

> *Son:* Mom, which way will you vote this election?
>
> *Mother:* For Clinton, of course.
>
> *Son:* Have you always voted Democratic, Mom?
>
> *Mother:* Oh, no. When we lived on the West Side of Chicago we always voted Republican.
>
> *Son:* Did you like Republican candidates, then?
>
> *Mother:* Oh, no. But everyone in that ward was a Democrat. We had to vote Republican.
>
> *Son:* What happened when you moved to the suburbs?
>
> *Mother:* Oh, in DuPage County they were all Republicans. We had to vote Democratic.

The dark side of human potential, including what has been called madness, can enrich the social matrix. American culture has been enriched by the separate and unique community of Anabaptists. Many useful programs have come from the Anabaptists, such as the Heifer Project and Church World Service. But *being* the dark side, rather than *having* one, can create a rigidity that is difficult to overcome.

·5·

To Heal the Broken

Healing

The style of healing in Anabaptist circles has varied from generation to generation and community to community: medicine, surgery, natural remedies, chiropractic, baths, shamanism, community health, and community trust. But Anabaptism does have one common thread in its understanding of healing: illness has not been caused by personal sin. Protestants have often connected ill health with punishment for sin. Since Anabaptists have no doctrine of original sin and tend to look on all of creation as good, they are free to see disease as an unfortunate event in the course of life. It would be hard to determine exactly why, but early medical people among the Anabaptists were accustomed to taking case histories like classical physicians and to seeking natural, rather than supernatural, causes.[1] As a consequence, some Anabaptist physicians, especially Hutterites, were widely sought for their skills in medicine. *The Chronicle of the Hutterian Brethren* offers a short notice on one of the most famous:

> His Imperial Majesty Emperor Rudolf II had been suffering from a dangerous disease for a long time, unable to make any recovery, although many famous medical doctors from Italy, Spain, and other countries attended him. Finally in that year of 1581 he sent for our doctor, brother Georg Zobel, to come to him at Prague in Bohemia. The emperor listened to his advice, accepted the treatment he suggested, and recovered. Through God's help he grew well and strong. Our doctor Zobel, who attended him for six months, was then sent home with a friendly farewell. Some nobles said the emperor would have died if our doctor had not come.[2]

Zobel was not only respected by nobility but held in high regard by the sisters and brothers of the Hutterite community. In 1593 they elected him *Diener der Notdurf* (chief steward) of his community, and later a *Hof* (the

German term for the location of a Hutterite community) named Zobelhof appeared in Hungary.

From the Nikolsburg Hof in Moravia yet another physician received high acclaim. In 1606, after thirteen years of war, Austria and Turkey ratified a peace agreement, and when, in 1608, the imperial embassy traveled from Austria to Constantinople, a Hutterite, Balthasar Goller, was asked to accompany the ambassador as his personal physician. Goller was also the personal physician for Franz Cardinal Dietrichstein; Dietrichstein was in charge of the counter-Reformation in Moravia, which included persecuting the Hutterites. Historians are not certain how Goller managed to serve so faithfully his own people's persecutor.[3]

The *Chronicle* mentions a number of other physicians among the Hutterites. The unusually large number of "caregivers" among the Anabaptists still remains something of a mystery. It seems highly unlikely that Hutterites or other Anabaptists would have encouraged the kind of education required for so many doctors. In the beginning decades physicians were surely converts. The convert shared the simple lifestyle and turned over his earnings to the community. (Of course, physicians could easily be independent of the community, so they must have, from time to time, exhibited more individuation than others, and there are intimations, at least, that some barber-surgeons were taking financial advantage of the Hutterite communities.) Why would doctors join the Hutterites?

Unlike other physicians who attached ill health to sin, Hutterian physicians sought natural causes and offered natural cures. Indeed one suspects some connection between Anabaptist healing and the famous contemporary physician Paracelsus. Paracelsus lived (better stated, wandered) in Austria and eastern Switzerland during the first half of the sixteenth century. He was an outspoken radical genius. Although he attended and graduated from the university, he said quite openly that he had learned more about medicine from the common folk. Because of this association with common folk, especially miners of the Villach region, he could advocate the use of natural minerals and chemicals for the curing of diseases. While he is known as the father of pharmacology, his methods parallel the Anabaptist practice of homeopathy. Paracelsus never became an Anabaptist, but his lifestyle, theological writings, and sermons have much in common with the radical reformation.[4]

Did the Anabaptists, especially the Hutterites with their separate communities, offer a unique medical opportunity for physicians who shared the convictions of a Paracelsus? Do we find in the left wing of the

Reformation a medical breakthrough? Do we find an approach to religion and health that broke with the medieval synthesis? We may see here the beginning of a particular concern for healing that leads to modern-day Anabaptist wellness programs, concerned as they are with cause instead of cure.

At that time European physicians were divided into three types: the *Artz*, a doctor who was more a theorist than a clinician; the *Chirug*, a surgeon with academic credentials; and the *Bader*, the barber-surgeon who cut hair, ran baths, and offered such popular medical remedies as bloodletting (phlebotomy) and cupping. Most of the doctors mentioned in the Hutterian *Chronicle* were *Bader*, and the Hutterites apparently were quite well known for their *Badelhäuser*, or bath houses. At least one angry opponent of the Hutterites, a pastor by the name of Christoph Andreas Fischer, was scandalized by the popularity of the Hutterian *Bader:*

> Not only the common man, but even the lords, when they are in need of any sort of treatment, run to [Hutterite] physicians as though they were the ones who had gobbled up the whole art of medicine. How can the unskilled Anabaptists accomplish such things? There is more to dancing than wearing red slippers. They have already caused the death of many of my parishioners who put their lives into their hands.[5]

Despite the speculation that Anabaptist communities, with their doctrine of goodness, may have offered a revolutionary context for sixteenth-century physicians, we have little information today about early Anabaptist medical practices. The Hutterites did run schools and baths, and instructions that have been preserved from these institutions indicate somewhat obliquely the health concerns of Anabaptists. Since these *Schul-Ordnung* are not well known, I will quote at length from one dating from 1578. One notices the emphasis on cleanliness (well before Pasteur) and the unusual kindness and understanding shown to the children (well before Spock).

> Herein are recorded several necessary points which the brethren and sisters who are appointed to supervise the schools, together with their assistants, are to observe in the care and discipline of the youth.
>
> In the first place they must constantly keep in mind that they are appointed over the children by the Lord and by His people.
>
> . . . .
>
> They shall take care that no disunity, strife, or boisterous speaking is heard by the children, but rather by a peaceful, cheerful, good-natured and

sober life and quiet walks they shall inspire the youth likewise to quiet and sober living and give them a good example.

. . . .

In the morning the girls shall be called at five o'clock in winter to spin. Then at six o'clock the boys are to be awakened and while the latter are dressing, combing, and washing, the smaller children are to be taken out, dressed, and washed, and after they have had a bit of exercise and been walking about they may be taken to their meals, so that they are not fed at once after awakening from sleep which is unnatural.

. . . .

The brethren in the schools have already been instructed by the elders that they shall not manifest wrath toward the children and shall not strike the children on the head with the fist nor with rods, nor shall they strike on the bare limb, but moderately on the proper place.

. . . .

The bed clothing shall be kept clean and shall be regularly changed, and when little children arise in the morning a sister or two or three girls must always be at hand to take care on the stairways that no one falls.

When the children are brought to the school they should be carefully examined and if any one is found to have a contagious disease such as scurvy or French disease [syphilis] or *lem*, the same should be instantly separated from the rest in sleeping and drinking and particularly in washing. Also special brushes and combs shall be used in taking care of the hair of those having skin eruptions. Those who have such eruptions shall be put together and not kept with those who are clean. Likewise those who have head diseases. If a child suffers or receives an injury on account of carelessness of whatever sort it may be, the injury shall not be concealed, but help and counsel shall be sought as soon as possible before greater injury comes of it.

And when the school mothers examine the children for bad mouths and reach into a bad mouth with the fingers, they shall be careful that they do not at once with unwashed fingers reach into a healthy mouth and thereby contaminate it, but shall always beforehand cleanse the fingers with a clean cloth and water before they examine and cleanse mouths. They shall likewise demonstrate to the sisters with them how to heal scurvy of the mouth, and not withhold this from them that others also may be able to attend to such things if they are appointed for it.

. . . .

In the case of the diseased heads and bad mouths the school mother shall take especial care, in particular about contagious diseases, and shall arrange for a separation in all matters, as in part already stated, as for instance in the matter of beds, washing, eating, drinking, using spoons and cups, also in the matter of examining the mouth and sitting on stools.

Once a week the clothes of the children shall be examined for lice, likewise the clothes of the children when they come to school. The new children shall have their heads and clothing examined for lice.

. . . .

One should not let the shoes of the children become too hard so that they cause blisters and the parents may have occasion for complaint. Therefore care should also be taken that the clothing and everything else is regularly repaired.

. . . .

The food which is to be given to the children they shall not be forced to eat. Drinking shall also be attended to so that drinking is not postponed too long or refused so that the thirst does not become so great that they drink to excess, which is harmful.

And for the sick children especially one should be free to ask the cook for that which they may need; yet this should be done orderly and not each sister run to the cook on her own account, but the request should be made on advice of the school mother.

When children are sick one should not be too severe with them if they ask for this or that, but should in true faithfulness as unto God be diligent in waiting upon them, in lifting and laying down in cleaning and washing.

. . . .

If a child will not keep quiet during the admonition it shall be taken out so that the other children may not become restless, for sometimes one child is itchy, another one thirsty, a third has some other need which one does not know. For this reason it is not possible to bring everything in order by using the rod.

. . . .

All this which has been written and told at some length is a pattern of how counsel should be given to those who are concerned with the schools. At times more should be said and at times less, just as is necessary at each place according to the circumstances. By this each one will know how to conduct himself so that the honor of the Lord may be promoted.[6]

Ten years before this instruction manual appeared, a chief bishop addressed a group of school masters with these words of advice:

Also, you, together with the sisters, must pay attention to the shoes which make the feet sore. Where shoemakers are at hand you should have the shoes frequently repaired and greased so that they will be nice and soft and so that not too many shoes are bought, as has happened in some cases and afterward they become too small or are spoiled.

Further, you should yourselves sleep with the children and should be present when they get up and should yourselves look after putting the children to bed and not rely altogether upon the bedroom maid. You should make sure that the children who are well are kept together and those who are not well are kept together. The same caution should be taken to keep those together who have eruption and make sure that the bed clothing for such is washed separately by itself.

Further, in regard to the children who are not well, or where there is uncertainty, the bed clothing and night shirts of such should not be mixed with the clothing of the children or washed together with it. It should be kept by itself. Likewise in the food and drink one cannot take too much care, for there is very much danger among so many children. The same thing is true in regard to washing and bathing, the two should not be mixed. You must take care and watch carefully to bathe and wash the unclean children by themselves. You must take care yourself that the sisters do not make the water for bathing too hot for the children. You should feel with your own hands whether it is not too hot, and if it is too hot you should forbid the sisters to use it, for it has often been the case that the skin of the children has become red like a crab and yet they would say: "why that is not too hot; you are not to bother yourself about such things." But you must not pay attention to such remarks.

Further, if a child has eczema, you should not let it be bathed or washed so often. It often has happened that although a child reported this ailment, nevertheless it has been compelled to bathe, and it was told: "Oh, that will not hurt you, you bad boy, or bad girl."

Further, you should not bathe the children every fortnight, for this is not necessary, but bathe them once in four weeks and wash them every fortnight, unless there is a special reason or on account of bad heads.[7]

While we are struck by the extraordinary kindness and patience shown to the children, even more striking is the philosophy behind such treatment: health problems have a natural cause, and such problems should be treated in a reasonable, natural manner. Or, to put it another way, there are no supernatural causes and no supernatural cures. Alchemy and magic are missing. The schools followed almost modern sanitary practices and very advanced principles of child training. To be sure, the medical practices of later centuries are not present here, nor even Anabaptist wellness programs, but the *Schul-Ordnung* of the first Hutterites does prefigure a time when health will be a matter of reasonable and patient reflection. Little wonder everyone wanted a Hutterite doctor! Our ministerial critic Fischer could hardly contain his anger over this turn of events: "The puffed-up physicians (*Bader*) ride up and down through the countryside. Every Saturday their baths are packed full of Christians [Roman Catholics]. And not alone the common people, but also the big shots come running to them if they ever need treatment as if the Anabaptists were the only ones who possessed this art in the entire region."[8]

From the sixteenth and seventeenth centuries until this century we know little more about the practice of medicine in Anabaptist circles. But intimations of a later time can be seen as Anabaptism spread throughout the world. Dutch Mennonites developed a system of deaconesses that had wide influence in caregiving. The Dutch deaconesses were not nurses, per se, but women ordained to take responsibility for the care of the poor and needy. Their projects included homes for older women, orphanages, and homes for mentally handicapped children.

Mennonites who immigrated to Russia took with them the same practices of folk medicine and the same patient care found in northern Europe. There were few physicians. Children were delivered by midwives, albeit not terribly successfully — at the end of the nineteenth century in one Russian settlement the infant mortality rate rose to nearly 30 percent. Despite shortcomings, concern for all members of the community was everywhere present. Children who were mentally handicapped, deaf, or epileptic received twice the inheritance that healthy siblings received. The extra funds were used to support institutions for handicapped children. By the end of the nineteenth century Russian Mennonites had developed homes for the aged, orphanages, a school for the deaf, a hospital for mental illnesses, and even a school for the deaconess-nurses.[9]

Midwifery continued into American Anabaptist life. A Mennonite woman, Bessie Hailey of Stuarts Draft, Virginia, wrote this reflection about three midwives in her Virginia community (Betty Treavy Brydge, 1848–1937; Isabelle Henderson Brydge, 1871–1961; and Osa Henderson, 1871–1953):

> We had little contact with other churches, as transportation was walking or driving horse and buggy. We lived about ten miles from another Mennonite Church. There were about 17 families in a radius of two miles. When children were born, these three women acted as mid-wives. They took care of the delivery, washing, dressing, feeding and looked after the mother for several days. In fact, the mother stayed in bed for ten days. The nearest doctor was twelve miles away and could only be reached when someone rode horseback to his office. He in turn, had to drive a horse and cart to see the patient. This changed somewhat about 1915 when my father had a telephone put in our home, and the neighbor folks used this to call a doctor. Medicine used was camphor, wormseed oil, calomel, soda, catnip tea, epsom salts, liniments, sassafras tea, etc. Mothers nursed their babies. These three women would see about giving the medicine to the children

in the neighborhood. Also sat up at nights and made clothes for the needy children, as they had no time in the daytimes, as they were busy doing things for their own families.[10]

The Pennsylvania Dutch culture of North America leaned heavily toward folk medicine, natural cures, and shamanism. Although some Anabaptists are puzzled by Pennsylvania "powwowing," it follows the original pattern — natural cures and community support. It is true, however, that superstitions crept in and the shamans reintroduced supernaturalism. Brethren probably differed somewhat from Mennonites in this regard. Though there were some shamans among the Brethren, there was also a tradition of elder-physicians. One of the most famous was the heroic Elder John Kline of Linville Creek, Virginia (1797–1864), who constantly crossed military lines and rendered medical aid to both Northern and Southern soldiers during the Civil War. He eventually was ambushed and killed as a traitor because he treated Union soldiers. Besides being a minister (in the Church of the Brethren the highest degree of ministry at that time was the elder, or presbyter), Kline acted as a country doctor. He advocated natural remedies and the use of herbs, following the medical system of Dr. Samuel Thompson. With this method he could give medical assistance to many while avoiding such popular cures as bloodletting, cupping, blistering, drastic cathartics, and starvation.

Another remarkable example of the elder-physician type can be seen in three generations of the Fahrney family. Peter Fahrney (1767–1837) served the area of southern Pennsylvania and northern Maryland; he was known at the time as the "walking doctor" who specialized in herbal treatments. His son Jacob Fahrney (1798–1848) served as an elder in the Church of the Brethren and as a physician. Jacob's son, Peter (1840–1905), in turn received medical and pharmaceutical instruction, and he eventually made a fortune with proprietary (patent) medicines. He was best known for his "Dr. Peter's Blood Cleanser or Panacea."[11]

Despite such sidetracks into folk medicine, by the end of the nineteenth century Mennonites and Brethren, like other denominations, had embraced a strong program of medical missions. Mennonites started missions in Indonesia and then spread to many Third World countries. Brethren started work in Africa and India.

The establishment of Anabaptist mission hospitals follows a pattern. North American doctors and nurses are sent to the mission location. They start a hospital with the assistance of indigenous personnel. The Western missionaries run the hospital, receive medicine and funds from North America, employ native assistants, assist in their training, and eventually turn the hospital over to the local people (or governments).

A Brethren hospital in Castañer, Puerto Rico, would be a good example of the Anabaptist pattern.[12] Conscientious objectors during World War II tried to do relief work in China but were prohibited from doing so by the U.S. government. Instead, then, the "volunteers" chose an isolated, mountainous village in Puerto Rico. A plot of land was obtained near the center of the town, and a school and a small clinic built. The school and clinic were owned, directed, and staffed primarily by U.S. Brethren fulfilling their term of alternative service. Very soon the school became the town's own. A Brethren church was built near the hospital on the original plot of land. In 1980 the hospital was handed over to a local board of directors, and in 1986 the land was so divided that the hospital and its local directors held title to their land, while the church held title to its parcel. In 1992 the hospital, along with the town and members of the Church of the Brethren, celebrated fifty years of service to the community.

In addition to this kind of service or mission hospital, Hutterites and Mennonites sometimes created another type of medical service. Having formed a colony or settlement in a "distant" land, they frequently established a hospital within the colony. Since the colonies were usually founded in remote areas, these hospitals often offered the only medical service available for miles. In 1928, for example, Mennonite immigrants, primarily from Russia and Canada, settled in Paraguay. Many were already ill (and therefore had been refused admittance to Canada), and the trip to Paraguay only exacerbated their health problems. A doctor sent by the Mennonite Central Committee determined that three-quarters of the settlers had trachoma and half had hookworm. After a hospital was constructed by the settlers, North American Mennonites sent medical personnel. Eventually nursing training was established, and basic medical skills like pharmacology and anesthesiology were taught. Promising youth were sent to Asunción for more technical training. Recently the Mennonites worked with the government of Paraguay to establish leprosy clinics.

The Bruderhof (an intentional Christian community that eventually joined with the Hutterites) also established a settlement in Paraguay, called Primavera. They had entered Paraguay because of persecution in Germany at the beginning of World War II. Health, of course, was an immediate concern for these refugees. With the help of Mennonites, Brethren, and Quakers a hospital was built in the *Hof* called Loma Hoby. The hospital served more Paraguayans than settlers, especially on an outpatient basis.

For reasons not entirely clear Anabaptists have built very few general hospitals in North America. Communal settlements have their clinics, of course, but Mennonites have concentrated their energies on developing a fine system of mental health hospitals, while both Brethren and Mennonites have developed superior homes for the elderly.

Mutual aid, as such, is discussed below, but I will say a word about health insurance here. In nations where there is an adequate health insurance system (Canada, Germany, the Netherlands), Anabaptists tend to let members participate in the state system. But where insurance is needed, Anabaptists have frequently developed their own insurance systems, called "aid societies." In 1902 the Menno-Friendly Beneficial Association was formed in Philadelphia at the First Mennonite Church for the purpose of giving relief "to members who shall be confined to their homes by reason of sickness or disability or accident." The most prominent of Mennonite aid institutions, Mennonite Mutual Aid (MMA, in Goshen, Indiana), was formed in 1949 as a means of providing health care for its members. Its programs go far beyond what I have described to this point. MMA even has a comprehensive proposal for reforming U.S. health care delivery. Brethren also formed a mutual aid society (the Brethren Mutual Aid Society in Abilene, Kansas), but this beneficial group has leaned toward property rather than health insurance. Health insurance has been available to church workers from Benefit Trust of Elgin, Illinois.

Caring

The family of Anabaptists has several striking characteristics, such as pacifism, volunteerism, and a communal frame of reference. But to the world at large perhaps nothing is more striking than its caring. Anabaptist groups have produced caring projects that far exceed what could be expected from such small denominations. It is useful to consider the roots of such caring and its implication for the stance of the Anabaptist tradition toward the linking of faith and health.

Theologically speaking, Anabaptists will bypass theory in favor of praxis every time. Christianity is much more a matter of life than a matter

of thought or belief. Anabaptists are seldom attracted to wrong thinking, but belief systems are not something about which they often reflect
or talk. Following the prophets and the sayings of Jesus, Menno Simons
emphasized the lived nature of true faith:

> The Almighty great God will not be satisfied with a bare name. He desires
> a true, sincere faith; unfeigned, ardent love; a new converted heart; true
> humility, mercy, chastity, patience, righteousness and peace. He desires the
> whole man: heart, mouth, and deed; men who delight in the Word of the
> Lord, speak the truth from the heart, crucify their flesh; men who will
> give, if need be, their goods and blood for the Word of the Lord.[13]

From the beginning Anabaptists took care of the poor and ill among
them. These acts were an extension of Christian love, and in the community of faith such care and love would only be natural. From the beginning
Anabaptists did not depend on society at large to care for its needy. Anyone
who has known the plain people of Pennsylvania, the Amish and Mennonites of Ohio and Indiana, cannot help noticing the way members of
these communities help each other; as Menno Simons wrote: "True evangelical faith cannot lie dormant....It clothes the naked. It feeds the hungry.
It comforts the sorrowful. It shelters the destitute. It serves those that
harm it. It binds up that which is wounded. It has become all things to
all men."[14]

The Brethren leader Michael Frantz makes care of others even more
explicitly an extension of the faith communion:

> If the inward communion with God has been truly realized, it will issue
> in outward communion..., with all kinds of virtues of love, for when the
> name of the word of congregation or communion is spoken in truth, then
> the words "mine" and "yours" must no longer be heard. That is to say
> [that] no one is to own or possess anything by himself any longer. To this
> extent "mine" and "yours" may be spoken on this basis, that this is mine
> and that is yours to administer and keep until a time of need for the poor
> and suffering in and outside of the congregation. To love one's neighbor
> as one's self shows clearly what communion is. Thus it behooves him who
> has two coats to give to him who has none, and he who has food, let
> him do the same (Luke 3). From this it is to be understood that he who
> has two portions, be it food or clothing, house, property, livestock, money
> or whatever his neighbor needs for his life's necessity, then love should
> compel him to give to his brother and to his neighbor and to do as he can
> for their need.[15]

Mutual Aid

All the Anabaptists are noted for mutual aid — that is, caring for one another within the community. So intense is this sense of caring that often persons raised in the Anabaptist tradition cannot easily function in the more individualistic Western society. Among communal types mutual support is implicit.[16] At a death the entire family will return home; the local community will care almost completely for the bereaved family and friends. At the time of a birth the community will care for the mother's family. Anything less would be unthinkable. If a family's breadwinner cannot work, the community of faith will bring in meals and offer assistance. If a young man has been refused a government student loan because of his objection to "swearing allegiance," the required loyalty oath, the community itself will make the loan. These are not ethical decisions. They are fundamental, spontaneous expressions of caring. In fact, even to suppose there is an intentional decision involved means one has lost the sense of community.

The Hutterite (and Amish) communities continue this intense, personal mutual aid to this day. While Mennonites and Brethren still practice local support, they also have institutionalized their mutual aid. Already by 1663 a group of Prussian Mennonites had organized a fire insurance association called Tiegenhöfer Privat Brandordnung, an association that endured until the communities were destroyed by the Russian invasion of Prussia (1945). A number of other property aid groups have been established over the years, now (since 1956) associated through the Association of Mennonite Aid Societies. Beyond property assistance, Mennonites also organized personal insurance, life insurance, health insurance, retirement plans, church building loans, investments, automobile insurance and loans, and other forms of mutual aid. In 1945 all of this aid was organized under a parent organization called Mennonite Mutual Aid. From this very active organization stem many of the wellness programs and health plans circulating among Mennonites and other groups concerned about health (including the Church of the Brethren).

The Brethren story does not differ greatly from that of the Mennonites. Brethren, too, practiced mutual aid among the members. And indeed there have been among the Brethren occasional intentional communities, the most famous of which was the Ephrata Community (founded in 1732 by Conrad Beissel). Other radical Pietistic communities included the Blooming Grove Colony in Lycoming County, Pennsylvania, and to some extent

Rapp's New Harmony in southern Indiana. Reba Place of Evanston, Illinois, represents for both Mennonites and Brethren a modern intentional community: since 1975 its members have pursued secular vocations while sharing their income, living in community housing, and participating in worship open to all. It would be safe to say that the radical Pietistic communities of the nineteenth century were more visionary and utopian than the earlier, more pragmatic Hutterite communities.

Brethren were so insistent on voluntary, informal mutual aid that, unlike the Mennonites, they not only shunned general societal welfare but also avoided mutual aid insurance. It was not until the late nineteenth century that Brethren were allowed to purchase property insurance, and not before 1920 that the Annual Conference of the Church of the Brethren allowed its members to purchase life insurance. Therefore, in contrast to the Mennonites, only a few mutual aid societies were formed: primarily the Brethren Mutual Aid Society (formed in 1885, after the 1879 Annual Conference decision to allow such mutual fire insurance companies among Brethren).

Brethren and Mennonites understood that caring meant care for one's neighbor. We have already seen that hospitals built in South America and the Caribbean also served the local communities. Much earlier the Mennonites of Russia gave considerable assistance to others in need. They aided the wounded during the Napoleonic invasion. During the Crimean War in their own communities they took care of five thousand sick and wounded soldiers. Exposure to the illnesses of the soldiers often brought death to the Mennonites who helped them. In the Russo-Japanese War Mennonite young men volunteered to aid sick and wounded soldiers.[17]

But it was not until this century, perhaps, indeed, not until World War II that Anabaptist service projects came into prominence. These projects are associated with the Mennonite Central Committee (MCC), and the Brethren Service Commission and its successor organizations.[18] On January 25, 1919, the first unit of relief workers sent by a Mennonite committee to a foreign relief project sailed out of New York on the *Pensacola* bound for Beirut.[19] The MCC itself began in 1920 as a structural way for international Mennonites to develop a Mennonite famine relief program in Russia. In 1930 it aided Russian Mennonites to resettle in Paraguay. It was in 1939 that MCC concerns shifted to projects for persons specifically other than Mennonites (the Mennonite Relief Commission for War Sufferers).

Like Mennonites, Brethren have long been involved in relief projects. In fact, the Brethren love feast served (as did the meal in the early church) as a locus for sharing food with needy neighbors.[20] Between 1788 and 1875 the minutes of Annual Meetings contain numerous instructions on caring for the poor who were not members of the congregation. During the Civil War Elder John Kline and others treated the sick and wounded of both sides, and the Annual Meetings of 1885 and 1886 approved collections to help those who still suffered from the war. In 1918 a Relief and Reconstruction Committee was formed to offer relief to people in Armenia, Syria, and eventually China. In 1937 the Historic Peace Churches, at the initiative of the American Friends Service Committee, collaborated in a relief program for victims of the Spanish Civil War. While historians do not all agree on this, many of us believe that the Brethren Service Commission started in Spain in 1939.

The magnitude of modern Anabaptist caring staggers the imagination. As we have seen, care for one's community is fundamental to the Anabaptist faith, yet around 1939 this commitment to co-religionists expanded and exploded into a global commitment to humanity. What happened? Many of us will say that something happened in Spain which triggered the historic peace churches into an outpouring of global care, but more sober historians will find another cause. Incredible as it may seem, the stimulus was the United States government.

Section 5(g) of the Selective Training and Service Act (1940) provided that registrants for the draft who were opposed "by reason of religious training and belief" to military duty should be assigned to "work of national importance under civilian direction." In 1941 the director of Selective Service was asked to establish such a program, known as Civilian Public Service (CPS).[21] Among the historic peace churches the American Friends Service Committee was responsible for negotiations with the United States government. Eventually the Brethren Service Commission and the Mennonite Central Committee assumed responsibility for most of the CPS programs. We have already seen that the experience of Mennonites and Brethren in mental hospitals gave rise to several excellent Mennonite mental health clinics. The experience of the peace churches with CPS and the Selective Service was not completely satisfactory. It was a compromise. After the war Mennonites and Brethren adapted CPS into an alternative service program for men of draft age and a volunteer service program for women and men. Many creative service programs grew out of the experience of these young people as they adjusted to difficult situations around the world.

As these programs developed, some distinguishing characteristics appeared among the peace churches. Without pressing the matter too closely, we can use these characteristics as useful clues for understanding the variations in the Anabaptist movement. The experience of the Mennonites, for whatever reasons, does not encourage governmental or even ecumenical cooperation. The Mennonites are best at acting more or less independently on their convictions or contributing personnel to compatible programs supported by other agencies. Brethren, on the other hand, have had a more satisfactory relationship with governmental agencies and ecumenical partners. Nearly all the Brethren programs have eventually resulted in cooperative programs.

Christ and Service

Brethren have a strong tendency to act on a humanitarian basis. While their relief assistance is not given anonymously (although it may be given through another agency and therefore by some name other than the Church of the Brethren), there is little effort to stress the Christ-like nature of the aid or the service offered. To be sure, most parcels sent overseas were marked by the cross and circle associated with the Brethren Service Commission, but, again, there was seldom any attempt to create communities of Brethren where the assistance was given. For many recipients the seeming informality of the giving did not at all match the value of the assistance received. Stories of such discrepancies abound among those who participated in the commission's projects.

In 1954 M. R. Zigler, a patron saint of the Brethren Service Commission, asked me if I wanted to accompany him as he gave a group of heifers to some German farmers near Kassel, Germany. Of course, I did. So we set out for the ceremony. Great as M. R. was otherwise, he knew hardly a word of German, so he took along his capable German secretary to do the translating. He stood up and said, "Well, a group of farmers in northern Indiana felt it would be a good thing to share what they had with you farmers here in Germany." The secretary translated, "Meine Damen und Herren, ich grüsse Sie im Namen unseres Herrn, Jesus Christus." (Ladies and gentlemen, I greet you in the name of our Lord, Jesus Christ.) M. R. said, "So these farmers decided to give each of you one of their heifers on the assumption you would pass the calf on to someone else." The secretary translated, "Bauern von der Kirche der Brüder in den USA, weil Gott Ihnen seine die Liebe durch seinen Sohn gezeigt hat, wollen Sie jetzt diese göttliche Gabe mit Euch teilen." (Because God has given of his love to them through his Son, farmers from the Church of the Brethren in the

USA would like to share that divine gift with you.)[22] Clearly the secretary felt a greater need to identify the theological underpinnings of this act of kindness than did M. R.

Mennonites, on the other hand, very early made it clear that assistance was given in the name of Christ. In 1940 a Canadian Mennonite, John E. Coffmann, was stationed in England to help needy children. He found himself distributing large quantities of clothing from North American Mennonites, and he was concerned that there was no Christian identification with the clothing. He wrote to Orie O. Miller, an executive of MCC, with the following suggestion:

> May we present a suggestion which has come to us which might be useful in promoting the cause of Christ, as we administer the clothing which is made and donated by our people. This is to have suitable labels prepared which could be attached to the garments as they are made or packed. The labels might be of paper or cloth, and bear the name of the Mennonite Central Committee. A little slogan, such as: "In the Name of Christ" should be included on the label and a place left or designated for marking the size of the garment or the age of person for whom it was made. There are brethren or sisters at home who could work out a suitable design for such a label and they could be printed and distributed to the various individuals who are making the clothing, and sewn on the garment.[23]

The idea was well received and thereafter the words "In the Name of Christ" appeared on almost everything distributed by MCC. And, in contrast to the experience of the Brethren, small congregations of Mennonites, many resulting from the service activity of MCC personnel, can be found in all parts of the world.

Mutual (Covenant) Love

Whether Mennonite or Brethren, most of the caring projects established by Anabaptists involve mutuality. It is difficult to determine whether this drive to mutuality derives from a common community development or from a specific theological conviction. A theology of the whole person dictates that mutuality depends on both formation experience and faith conviction. True as that may be, the faith conviction cannot be easily isolated. One would suspect that the faith conviction which leads to mutuality must lie in the Anabaptist understanding of love, and that may be the answer. In contrast to some thinkers within the Reformation, Anabaptists believed divine love by definition included human love. Divine love was not simply unrequited love (*agape*) or grace, nor was it the well-known indicative/imperative (a divine act elicits a human action). Divine love for us and our love for God are one moment. Anabaptists would argue that such love defines the biblical sense of covenant, what biblical scholars call covenant love. Anabaptists did absorb covenant love from the Bible, but, theologically speaking, Anabaptism in general and Brethren in particular were influenced also by the "federal" or "covenant" theology associated with theologian Johannes Cocceius (1648) and biblical scholars Campegius Vitringa and Johann Albrecht Bengel.[24] They had adjusted Reformed theology in such a way to emphasize even more the communitarian nature of the people of God. If covenant love defines our relationship to God, then we also relate to each other in covenant love.

The writings of Anabaptist thinkers abound with statements about love and mutuality, but they mean, for the most part, the mutuality of the faith community. Many Anabaptists still assume the major mark of Christian love appears in the barn raisings, the funeral dinners, financial support, care of orphans, and other ways of supporting each other. And that has much truth to it. But in this century some great visionaries like Harold Bender have tried to broaden the definition of love by linking it with discipleship.[25] Christians are persons who follow Jesus, and to follow Jesus means also to be persons of love. In a sense Bender's discipleship motif shifts to the more Pietistic sense of following in the footsteps of Jesus, what Brethren also call *Nachfolge*. The first of the Brethren, Alexander Mack, described the believer as a disciple: "Observe well, that the true believers and lovers of the Lord Jesus have always looked steadfastly and single-mindedly to their Lord and Master in all things. They follow Him gladly in all of His commands, just as He has told them to do, and He has shown them by His own example."[26] It could well be that the redefinition of love through discipleship (for the Mennonites) and its rediscovery in *Nachfolge* (for the Brethren) did create the faith climate for the twentieth-century outpouring of care.[27] But such discipleship tends to lack the very mutuality of which we speak. Bender and other Mennonites could speak of nonresistance and sharing as mandates of discipleship regardless of the results. W. Harold Row and other Brethren would speak of a peace witness that had to be forcefully articulated whether or not it was politically feasible. Discipleship describes well the nature of obedience but tends to overlook responsibility for the consequences.

In the last few years some Anabaptist/Mennonite thinkers like Gordon

Kaufmann, J. Lawrence Burkholder, and Ron Sider have called for a responsible discipleship. On the Brethren side Ralph Smeltzer has insisted that Brethren involved in the civil rights movement should be fully aware of the consequences of their actions. In both groups today one would expect most leaders to speak of a love that has political and social awareness, rather than a love that "blindly" follows Jesus.[28]

Despite these reflections one cannot easily claim that mutuality in caring has derived from a love based on responsible discipleship. It would be tempting for a theologian to argue that Anabaptist theologizing shifts first from covenant love to community mutual aid, then to radical discipleship, and finally, in our time, to responsible global caring.[29] One could also argue that the movement of mutual aid toward a global scope simply reflected what had been learned through centuries of life in community. While there are faith components to such mutual caring, a one-to-one relationship between faith and action, between theory and praxis, cannot ever be ascertained. In fact, the theological formulations almost surely resulted from changes in praxis. It would be wiser to say that the experiences of World War II so affected Anabaptists as to create a global perspective that resulted in remarkable global projects, and at the same time opened the way for a theology of responsible, universal mutuality. Anabaptism of the twenty-first century will build on the changes that began in 1939.

The nature of Anabaptist mutual caring can be easily stated. In blighted areas of Africa, for example, Anabaptists would be more likely to help people build wells than to donate food (though they would do that, too). The Christian Rural Overseas Project (CROP), for example, which was initiated by Brethren I. W. Moomaw and M. R. Zigler and eventually sponsored by the Church World Service in 1947, not only sent food to war-torn Europe and Japan but also provided the means to self-help: tools, well-drilling equipment, windmills, seed, and the like.[30] In cases of natural disaster Anabaptists will more likely send teams of construction workers to help local families rebuild than give money for lumber. When Mennonites give aid they may well develop a faith community that will continue the witness of mutual caring. Brethren will likely develop a local committee that can continue the program. Some examples will make clear the Anabaptist commitment to service.

Heifer Project

The famous Heifer Project is a good illustration of Anabaptist caring.[31] When Brethren visionary Dan West served as a relief worker with the American Friends Service Committee during the Spanish Civil War, he was deeply struck by the suffering of the Spanish people. He was particularly dismayed by the failure of powdered milk to sustain life and feed the children. When he returned to his home in northern Indiana, a land flowing with milk if not honey, he proposed to his Brethren neighbors that they find a way to share their dairy cattle with the people of Spain or any others who lacked sufficient nutrition. The proposal was fairly well received, but it was not until 1942 that "Heifers for Relief" was officially approved by the Brethren of northern Indiana and the Brethren Service Commission.

The war in Spain was over, but World War II was at its fiercest level. West and the Brethren had a program, but nowhere to go. Because overseas shipment of cattle was difficult in any case and impossible during the war, the Brethren shipped their animals to sharecroppers in the United States, to Puerto Rico (where the offspring can still be seen today), and to Mexico. As World War II came to a close, the international community determined to help in the recovery of war-damaged areas. The United Nations Relief and Rehabilitation Administration (UNRRA) was formed for that purpose. UNRRA agreed to ship Heifer Project cattle if the Brethren could furnish attendants; the Brethren Service Commission agreed, and hundreds of Brethren became what were called "sea-going cowboys." *Time* magazine printed the following account:

> Baltimore stockyards rang with the impatient bellows of 337 cows, the whinnies of 396 restless mares. A ship stood empty in the harbor, ready to load. And across the water, Yugoslavia, Poland, Greece, Albania, and Czechoslovakia (with more than five million farm animals lost in the war) waited hungrily for replacements. But UNRRA was stumped. The ship was ready. The animals were ready. But there were no livestock hustlers to herd the beasts overseas.
>
> Into the breach stepped brisk, friendly Benjamin G. Bushong, dairy farmer, cemetery owner, and chief red-tape cutter of the 226-year-old pacifist Church of the Brethren ("Dunkers" — because they practice baptism by total immersion). For months Dunker Bushong had been pushing his church's own overseas relief program (*Time*, July 24, 1944), only to strike a snag. City Dunkers had raised money for calves and feed. Country Dunkers had fed and fattened the animals into fine bulls and heifers. The Dunkers had the cattle but no ships. Dunker Bushong made a suggestion: if UNRRA would provide shipping space for Dunker cows and bulls, the Brethren

would rustle up seagoing hustlers to herd the UNRRA animals. UNRRA was delighted and agreed to pay volunteers $75 monthly expenses, token salaries of 1¢ daily. Expediter Bushong promptly rallied his people and submitted to volunteers what is probably the war's shortest, most to the point questionnaire: "Who are you? What can you do?" He picked 100 (preachers, teachers, students, and a shrewdly chosen handful of veteran dirt farmers) as herders.

Last week UNRRA was busy fulfilling its half of the bargain. As 100 more Dunker volunteers set sail for Europe, six fat Dunker Brown Swiss bulls were safe in Greece, 150 Dunker heifers awaited passage to Poland. Said pleased Pacifist Bushong: "Perhaps shootin' isn't the only way out of this world mess."[32]

The mutual nature of the Heifer Project is obvious, even ingenious. The heifer was ready to calve. Its milk, not its beef, would be used to feed the children, and the first calf would be given to yet another needy family. Before farmers could receive a heifer, they had to make this agreement about the firstborn. The Heifer Project was very successful. In a short time the sharing of animals extended to chickens and goats, with the same type of mutuality. In 1948, with the termination of UNRRA, an interfaith committee took over the Heifer Project. Members included the Brethren Service Commission, the Mennonite Central Committee, the American Baptist Churches, the Evangelical and Reformed Church (later the United Church of Christ), the Methodist Commission on Overseas Relief, the Rural Life Association, and the National Catholic Rural Life Conference. Under the guidance of the ecumenical committee, projects expanded to include sheep, pigs, rabbits, and bees, and assistance has been given to people in over one hundred countries.

Church World Service

The center of relief activity for the Brethren Service Commission was the facility in New Windsor, Maryland. It had been used to collect, store, and ship assistance to those who needed relief — victims of war or disasters. In 1946 M. R. Zigler, representing BSC, urged all Christian relief agencies to combine their efforts. This resulted in the formation of a large umbrella agency that encompassed various denominational efforts, the Overseas Relief and Rehabilitation of the (then) Federal Council of Churches, the Church Committee on Relief in Asia, and the World Service Committee of the World Council of Churches. The new agency was called Church World Service and is now the largest agency of the National Council of Churches.

The Brethren center in New Windsor (with auxiliary locations in Nappanee, Indiana, and Modesto, California) became a primary source for this new ecumenical agency.

Voluntary Service

Following World War II the Brethren decided to continue the program of service work for conscientious objectors. In contrast to policy during the war period, postwar conscientious objectors were allowed to do their service overseas. A large number of Brethren young men and women (about four thousand by 1980) were trained for volunteer service and sent around the world to assist other agencies in their service programs. One Mennonite group, the Mennonite Church, had authorized a volunteer service program as early as 1943, but like its Brethren counterpart, the Mennonite long-term service projects did not get under way until 1948. Shortly after the development of long-term volunteer service, the historic peace churches began to explore how volunteer agencies might relate to the government. W. Harold Row of the BSC chaired this committee until 1952 when the International Voluntary Services agency (IVS) was formed and a staff of Brethren personnel was secured. The federal government agreed to let IVS employ conscientious objectors and utilize volunteers in international development projects. IVS became the prototype for the Peace Corps, and in many respects has been superseded by the Peace Corps, although young men of the historic peace churches never were granted conscientious objector credit for Peace Corps service.

Sale of Handcrafts

When relief workers returned from the refugee camps in Germany, they often brought back handcrafts to give to their friends. Eventually they began to sell these handcrafted items and send back the proceeds to the refugees who had made them. In 1949 the Brethren set up a shop in New Windsor to sell items made primarily by refugees in German and Austrian refugee camps. Under BSC this was expanded to include the impoverished in several countries, but the project was named after its first intent: Sales Exchange for Refugee Rehabilitation Vocations (SERRV). In the early 1960s, in order to increase both the market and the contacts, the manager of SERRV arranged to work with Church World Service. By 1981 this project reported gross sales of $2.5 million for products coming from forty-three countries.

Much like the Brethren experience, the Mennonite project called SELF-HELP began when MCC workers returned with needlework items made by impoverished Puerto Ricans. The selling of such items remained a private enterprise until 1962, when MCC adopted it as a relief program. Having started as a full-fledged mutual care program in 1971, by 1987 SELFHELP also had gross sales of over $2 million.

Victim-Offender Reconciliation Program

All the Anabaptist groups are peace oriented. The historic peace churches generally include all the Mennonite groups, the Church of the Brethren, and the Quakers. The mutuality of love lies deep in the sense of reconciliation. Anabaptists do not intend to stop wars or fights, nor do they intend to bargain for peace or justice, but they intend to restore mutual relationships. The central meaning of reconciliation is to "overcome enmity."[33] While both Mennonites and Brethren historically have stressed reconciliation and can claim reconciling heroes and heroines, the Mennonite churches have worked more seriously at the task of overcoming enmity.[34]

There are many examples of Anabaptist reconciliation programs. A look at some of them will indicate once again the conviction of mutual love and peace which will, perforce, permeate all of Anabaptist life and, in particular, its view of health. The Victim-Offender Reconciliation Program (VORP) started among Mennonites in Kitchener, Ontario. It was the result of a joint program between volunteer probation workers and the MCC. The first case began in 1974 when two young men, while under the influence of alcohol, caused damage totaling $2,200 to twenty-two victims. The judge agreed to use a third-party facilitator who would attempt to achieve restitution for the victims and reconcile them to the offenders. After six months everyone was satisfied. In the United States the program first started in Elkhart, Indiana (a Mennonite stronghold). Also known as Prisoner and Community Together (PACT), the victim-offender reconciliation program has spread to a number of locales in the United States. VORP offers an excellent model of the Anabaptist sense of reconciliation. Mennonite volunteer Earl Sears narrates the following case from his work in VORP:

> After leaving a local bank, John Horne drove into the auto wash to have his car washed. He had $100 in a bank cash envelope lying on his front seat. When he pulled into the car wash he stopped and got out of the car

so that one of the employees could drive the car through the wash. In the process, the employee saw the envelope and stuck it in his pants cuff. As soon as he was done with the car, he went into the bathroom and hid the money, retrieving it later that evening.

Immediately upon picking up his car at the other end of the wash, Horne realized that the money was gone. He went directly to the management and told them what had happened. They called the police and within the next several days all of the persons who had been working at the time were questioned. Finally Bill Krepps, a 16-year-old employee, admitted that he had taken the money and that he had already spent it to buy a new stereo set.

The case was sent to the juvenile probation department who referred it to VORP. I was the volunteer assigned this case. I first contacted Krepps by phone to ask him about the possibility of talking with him about the case. He was very agreeable and we met one evening about 4:40 at his apartment, where we sat and talked for awhile. He showed me a stereo set that he had, although he didn't say then that it was the one he had purchased with the money.

We talked about the case. I explained to him that I would like to get John and him to sit down together to talk. He seemed very agreeable and willing to do this, although he did admit some fear and hesitation about it. I told him I would see John, explain to him the situation and see if he was willing to meet with us.

Within the next two days I made contact with John by phone and asked if I could visit him at his house. He agreed and that same evening at about 4:30 I stopped at his house. His house is located in a rather nice residential area. As I entered his house I noticed that his wife was lying in the living room in a hospital bed. He explained quickly that his wife had been an invalid for a number of years. As soon as I explained to him what we were trying to do, he told me how badly he needed the money and how upset he was with this young man. He implied that the young man who took his money might have been the kind of person from whom you would expect such activity.

We then talked further about the possibility that the three of us could talk about the whole experience. He told me that he wanted very much to have that money back because — and he pointed to his wife as he said this — "you can see that I am in need of all the money I can get, because it has been very expensive for us the last number of years."

John's first response was to say, "Why don't you simply go to Bill Krepps and tell him that he's got to pay me the money back?" He really was not sure he wanted to meet him because he did not think he would like to relate to that type of person. I assured him I understood his feelings. We talked further and again I encouraged him to consider the possibility of a meeting. I said in the past we have had meetings like this and they have been a good way to arrange for restitution. He reluctantly did agree to meet. The meeting was set for two nights later at his house.

I then left and called Krepps on the phone, confirmed the time and place with him and said I would pick him up. On the evening of the meeting Krepps was waiting for me and ready to go. When we were about halfway there he looked at me and said, "You know, I'm really scared to death. I hope this guy doesn't kill me." So I tried to assure him that Horne would not be the kind of person who would do any physical harm.

We arrived at Horne's house and I introduced the two. I told Horne that Krepps was now working at another car wash and also explained to Krepps that Horne had been taking care of his wife for the last number of years.

Then all three of us sat down in the living room. I had Krepps explain why he did what he did and how it happened. He very quickly said he was terribly sorry it had happened. He was the first one to get into the car, he saw the money and just on impulse he grabbed it; he never had any other reason. He assured Horne he had nothing against him as a person and he said it was the only time he had ever done anything like that.

Then Horne explained how he felt when he found the money gone. He said when he got into his car and saw the money was not there, he was very upset. He could not understand why Krepps would take it out of his car. Krepps again assured him it was just an impulse thing, he was sorry it happened and had nothing against John.

After further discussing their feelings, they agreed that if Krepps could pay back the $100, both of them would feel the case was resolved. Krepps said he could do that. He had $30 available and would pay Horne $10 a week until it would be paid off. Horne agreed.

I filled out the contract, had both of them sign it and at the end of the meeting explained to Horne that Krepps would pay the money to the probation department and then it would be sent to him. They both shook hands and Horne said to Krepps, "You know, you're a nice looking young man," implying that he was somewhat surprised Krepps would be involved in this kind of thing.

When we left Horne's house, I drove Krepps back home and he again indicated to me that he felt badly about the theft after he realized Horne's situation. Krepps did pay all of the $100. I contacted Horne after it was paid and he felt very good about what had happened.

I was pleased with this case because it seemed that both the victim and the offender had a change of attitude after the meeting. The offender realized afterwards that the car he robbed belonged to another person who had need for the money, particularly since he had an invalid wife. Earlier Krepps had told me he had always resented persons with money and felt that Horne's car and address indicated he could easily afford $100. But after the meeting Krepps realized that even Horne had financial needs.

The victim had believed the kind of person who would rob him was a certain kind of offender. When I had first met with Horne, he gave a clear indication that this was just one of the bad kids that you cannot trust. When the victim actually met him and heard him tell the story, he realized he was a young man who made a bad choice and a bad decision, but was not necessarily a totally bad kid. Horne was willing to say afterwards, "You know, you really seem like a nice kid to me. I hope that everything will work out for you in the future."

Consequently, I feel attitudes were changed on both sides and a healing took place between the victim and the offender that would likely not have happened in any other way. The face-to-face meeting did bring both to a new understanding that other persons are important and must be taken seriously.[35]

This case illustrates clearly and simply how the Anabaptist sense of mutual love strives for reconciliation rather than *agape* (Horne forgives Krepps and lets Krepps decide what to do) or justice (Krepps pays the court what is owed Horne and has a misdemeanor count filed against him). Horne and Krepps did not likely become friends, but surely Horne could take his car to Krepps's new place of employment, greet Krepps, and be certain nothing would be taken.

This case deals with a $100 theft. But Anabaptists are willing to play for much higher stakes. Their schools are offering formal training in reconciliation and peacemaking. In 1948 a Brethren college, Manchester (in Indiana), began the first college peace studies program. It dealt with the philosophy of peace, techniques of peacemaking, and conflict resolution. By 1986 three Mennonite colleges — Goshen (Indiana), Bethel (Kansas), and Conrad Grebel (Canada) — had also established departments of peace studies. Anabaptists who focus on peace studies have become more knowledgeable about world issues and more involved in global programs. Perhaps the ultimate prototype of this new breed of Anabaptists was Brethren minister and elder Andrew Cordier. Cordier taught at Manchester College and was a prime mover in the establishment of the peace studies department there. As executive assistant to the secretary-general of the United Nations from 1946 to 1962, Cordier was an extremely valuable advisor to leaders such as Dag Hammarskjöld and U Thant. In 1973 Cordier was nominated for the Nobel Peace Prize.

Today there are Anabaptist reconcilers around the world. In Cape Town, South Africa, Mennonite Ron Kraybill works with Professor Hendrik W. van der Merwe at the Centre for Intergroup Studies located in the University of Cape Town. His specialty is reconciliation between black and white South Africans. His center has made an agreement with Robert and Alice

Evans of Plowshares (Hartford, Connecticut) to train interracial reconcilers throughout South Africa — where all sides seem more concerned about
cultural and moral rectitude than a faith based on mutual love. Mennonite
Barry Hart works with Christian Health of Liberia to counsel with those
traumatized by civil war and to train persons in the art of reconciliation.
The list seems endless, but these current programs are offered merely as
samples of how Anabaptists have carried their sense of community and
mutual love into a global program of assistance and reconciliation.

·6·

Living in Hope

In you, O Father,
Is my joy,
Though I must suffer here!
Let me be scorned
By everyone
If your grace still is near.

And as, again,
Her time once come,
A woman bears her child in pain,
Then greets the new life
Full of joy and eagerly—
So we, too, suffer patiently.

For all who dared
His cross to bear,
A crown of joy Christ does prepare.
Their grief shall be
Turned to pure bliss and ecstasy
By Jesus Christ eternally.

God Father, Son and Spirit, too—
To them all praise and glory due
Be given by his people true.
Lord, lead your band
With gracious hand
Out of this world to your own land.

—Jeronimus Käls

Suffering

For the question of faith and health in the Anabaptist tradition few issues are more critical than that of suffering. It encompasses many other

facets of Anabaptist thought — martyrdom, persecution, Christology, use of
the Bible, and others — yet little has been written on the subject. Suffering is hardly mentioned in Brethren writings. In Hutterite and Mennonite
sources it does occur as a topic, but nearly always as a reflection on the
early martyr tradition. For Anabaptists suffering stems from following
Jesus. It may be redemptive because it shows that the one suffering is indeed a true disciple. It may also be disciplinary by calling the believer and
the faith community to more resolute faith. In any case, such suffering is
inevitable for a religious group that stands outside the mainstream.[1] Yet
there is no clear connection between the original sense of suffering as suffering with Christ (and the martyrs) and suffering in general. Anabaptists
have said little about theodicy, or about pain for the world's condition, or
about the pain of ill health.

The first Anabaptists understood themselves in terms of the Bible;
they understood their role in history in terms of the biblical people of
God and, most important, they understood their suffering in terms of the
cross. To say that the Bible, especially the New Testament, is the source
of Anabaptist faith may sound like obligatory pietism or even theological
romanticism. It is not. The biblicism of the early Anabaptists was fundamental. It must have staggered their persecutors and fascinated their
contemporaries. Take, for example, the remarkable disputation between
the interrogator Friar Cornelius and prisoner Jacob de Keersgieter (or
Jacob de Roore) on May 9, 1569:

> *Friar Cornelius:* Well, I've come here to see whether I can convert you
> (Jacob, I believe, is your name) from your false and evil belief, in which
> you are erring, and whether I cannot bring you back to the Catholic faith
> of our mother, the holy Roman church, from which you have apostatized to
> this damnable Anabaptism. What do you say to this, eh?
>
> *Jacob:* With your permission, as regards that I have an evil, false belief,
> this I deny; but that through the grace of God I have apostatized from your
> Babylonian mother, the Roman church, to the members, or the true church,
> of Christ this I confess; and thank God for it, who has said: "Come out of
> her, my people, that ye be not partakers of her sins, and that ye receive not
> of her plagues." Rev. 18:4; Isa. 52:11.
>
> *Fr. Corn:* Is it true? And do you call our mother the holy Roman church, the
> whore of Babylon? And do you call your hellish, devilish sect of Anabaptists
> the members, or the true church of Christ? Eh! hear this fine fellow once.
> Who the devil has taught you this! your accursed Menno Simons, I suppose,
> [obscene language omitted here].

Jac: With your permission, you talk very wickedly. It was not necessary that Menno Simons should have taught us as something new, that the Babylonian whore signifies your mother, the Roman church, since John teaches us enough concerning this in his Apocalypse, or Revelation, in the 14th, 16th, 17th and 18th chapters.

Fr. Corn: Ah bah! what do you understand about St. John's Apocalypse? at what university did you study? At the loom, I suppose; for I understand that you were nothing but a poor weaver and chandler, before you went around preaching and rebaptizing out here in the Gruthuysbosch. I have attended the university at Louvain, and studied divinity so long, and yet I do not understand anything at all about St. John's Apocalypse; this is a fact.

Jac: Therefore Christ thanked His heavenly Father, that He had revealed and made it known to babes, and hid it from the wise of this world, as is written, Matt. 11:25.

Fr. Corn: Exactly; God has revealed it to the weavers at the loom, to the cobblers on their bench, and to bellows-menders, lantern-tinkers, scissors-grinders, broom makers, thatchers, and all sorts of riff-raff, and poor filthy, and lousy beggars. And to us ecclesiastics who have studied from our youth, night and day, He has concealed it. Just see how we are tormented. You Anabaptists are certainly fine fellows to understand the holy Scriptures; for before you are rebaptized, you can't tell A from B, but as soon as you are baptized, you can read and write. If the devil and his mother have not a hand in this, I do not understand anything about you people.

Jac: I can well hear that you do not understand our way of doing; for you ascribe to Satan the grace which God grants our simple converts, when we with all diligence teach them to read.[2]

The letters and defense statements of the martyrs were replete with biblical quotes. The quotes were not prooftexts. Somehow the biblical passages enabled the first Anabaptists to join that first community of believers. It was a community of new joy but also a community of suffering.

At the center of Anabaptist biblicism was Christology. It was Jesus Christ who bridged the period of the two ages. The presence of Christ signaled the end of the old age, and his death and resurrection made possible the new age. As the one who ushered in the kingdom of God, Jesus suffered much. The account of the life of Jesus in *Martyrs' Mirror* points clearly toward the meaning of that suffering in the Anabaptist tradition. Indeed Jesus, the only and eternal Son of God, was born of the virgin Mary, in the town of Bethlehem. "But His entrance into this world, as well as His progress and end, was full of misery, distress and affliction, indeed it may be said: He was born under the cross; brought up under the cross! He walked under the cross, and finally died on the cross."[3] Jesus was born in great poverty, and by the time he was two the state (Herod) was trying to kill him. In the face of persecution and death the parents of Jesus took him to another country. As an adult Jesus was a vagrant, with no place to lay his head. At the end of his life he was betrayed by a friend and disciple for thirty pieces of silver, and his own people handed him over to the Romans, an oppressive occupying army. With the permission of the Romans, on the basis of trumped-up charges, he was mocked, tortured, and crucified. "He who died there was more than a common man, yea,...He was the Son of the living God. This, then, was the end, not of a martyr, but of the Head of all the holy martyrs, through whom they and we all must be saved."[4] Anabaptist Christology does not proclaim a divine sacrifice for our personal sins, does not describe a divine triumph over the principalities and powers, but speaks of a man who died to this age and came alive to the new age. All who truly follow Jesus will also suffer and as "martyrs" will be saved, that is, will also pass into the new age.

It would be going beyond the evidence to claim that Anabaptist Christology has followed the *Martyrs' Mirror* in its understanding of Jesus. Yet the qualities remain. Although we cannot claim that, for Anabaptists, Jesus *became* the Christ at the resurrection (was "declared to be Son of God with power according to the spirit of holiness by resurrection from the dead, Jesus Christ our Lord" [Romans 1:4]), the stress on Christ as the reconciler, rather than an ontological divine being, makes adoptionism nearly inevitable. By *adoptionism* we mean the belief that Jesus became the Christ *because* he was the firstborn of the martyrs, that is, through suffering he led us, his disciples, into the new age (*per crucem ad lucem*, through the cross to the light). Though not exactly the same as the discipleship or *Nachfolge* of the twentieth century, adoptionism still emphasizes that following Jesus entails suffering and leads to a new life and new society. Menno Simons writes about this believer's path of suffering in "The Cross of the Saints."[5] The arduous way of the follower of Jesus is a recurring motif in Anabaptist works; for example:

> O Herre Gott, der Weg, den bistu gangen,
> Der ist so schmal und ligt so voller Schlangen.
> [O Lord God, the path you have traveled
> Is so narrow and so full of snakes.][6]

Suffering discipleship involves several faith corollaries.

Two Kingdoms

Since the appearance of Augustine's *City of God*, it has been customary (rightly or wrongly) to divide the world into a kingdom of God and a kingdom of the state. The one seeks the will of God, the other seeks human good. One is based on love and the other on justice.[7] Christian traditions are often characterized by the way in which they deal with the two kingdoms. For example, it is said that in Eastern Orthodox Christianity the two are the same except that the church is the state at prayer. In Roman Catholicism the two are the same, except that the state is the church seeking justice. Protestants normally live in a much more complicated relationship between the two. Lutherans historically have the believer living in both at once, so the Lutheran must decide whether the church or the state has a dominant voice (or right) in any given issue.

Many Anabaptists simply split the two kingdoms apart. One lives in either the kingdom of God or the kingdom of the state, but not both, for the two kingdoms are envisioned as a *civitas dei* and a *civitas diaboli.* This conviction, of course, explains many things. It explains the Anabaptist's unwavering conviction that church and state must be separated, that the state cannot interfere with religious freedom (as in the cases of conscientious objection to war, Amish buggies on the road, Amish outhouses, and Native American peyote). It would be better for the people of the kingdom of God to avoid the technical developments of the kingdom of the state (television, electricity, automobiles) than to accept the values of a secular society.

Those who live in both kingdoms simultaneously endure a powerful dialectical tension. Questionable decisions can result in guilt and ill health. Those who live solely in the kingdom of God will face persecution and suffering, because their lifestyle, convictions, and values differ from those of society at large. All Anabaptist types understand that. Much suffering comes from the conflict between the two kingdoms. In fact, when they are not suffering, Anabaptists suspect that they are no longer rightly discerning the will of God. There is never a time to be at ease in Zion.

While all Anabaptists recognize the conflict between the two kingdoms, it would not be appropriate to say that they handle the conflict in the same way. Hutterites are more likely to solve the problem by establishing communities and colonies that depend on secular society as little as possible. Mennonites live more in society but try to limit the relationship. Both Hutterites and Mennonites recognize the state's legitimate function of maintaining justice. Brethren do not often speak of two kingdoms, and they are much more likely to expect society to be transformed. Brethren do not expect the state to preserve justice but expect society at large eventually to embrace the will of God. In fact, Brethren have a noticeable tendency to be universalists.[8]

The civitas diaboli. A favorite passage for Anabaptists is found in Paul's letter to the Romans: "Do not be conformed to this world [age], but be transformed by the renewing of your minds" (12:2a). Anabaptists understand the admonition not to be like this age and understand even more that this world and the desire for it are passing away (1 John 2:17). While Anabaptists seldom speak of an ontological dualism (two realities — one evil and one good), they often have perceived a cosmic dualism in which the powers of the old age are at war with the Lord of the new age. To Anabaptists, the secular powers are evil and are indeed passing away. One does not see here vengeance or vindictiveness. The old age simply will not last. In the register of martyrs of *The Chronicle of the Hutterian Brethren* one can see the awareness that all is not well for the persecutors. The rather gossipy register for 1527 and 1528 reads like this:

> Georg Wagner of Emmering was burned alive at Munich in Bavaria for the sake of his faith....The night the judge returned home from the execution, he met a sudden death. Three brothers and two sisters were executed at Znaim in Moravia. The judge wanted to arrest more brothers but great misfortune befell him. He became ill, cried out and bellowed like an ox, bit his tongue, and choked in blood.[9]

To be sure suffering in the early years sprang primarily from martyrdom and persecution. The Hutterian *Chronicle* and the *Martyrs' Mirror* tell the stories of suffering as the conflict between the two ages. Such stories construct self-identity. Anabaptists know who they are by telling stories of suffering and sacrifice.[10] Anabaptists did not and do not feel like victims because they know the suffering has meaning and that they stand in a long line of Christian martyrs. Yet sometime about 1939 the Anabaptist awareness of their own suffering as the persecuted of this world shifted to empathy for others who were victims; the *civitas diaboli* became an object of concern rather than merely a kingdom that was passing away. It was a critical shift, and we cannot easily predict what it means for the future of the Anabaptist tradition.

The civitas dei. With Jesus as the firstborn of all martyrs, the kingdom of God has come, and Jesus has become the firstfruits, the Son of God. Believers, by suffering with Christ, also gain access to the domain of God.

But access to the domain of God does not bring an end to the suffering. Quite the contrary. Anabaptists assumed with certainty that their historical fate would lead to martyrdom. The cross not only creates the way into the new age but guides the people of God in their new life together.

> Die Braut muss wie der Bräutigam
> Durch Leiden in die Freud eingahn.
> [Like the bridegroom, the bride
> goes into joy through suffering.][11]

Early Anabaptists took quite seriously their calling to fill out the sufferings of Christ (Colossians 1:24). While at first this suffering may have resulted from the conflict of the faith community with secular society, eventually Anabaptists took their suffering to be a redemptive activity worked out by God through them. Brethren Warren W. Slabaugh identified the church with the suffering servant of Isaiah.[12] Suffering was no longer a result of conflict with the state but the necessary characteristic of a church which cares and acts on that caring.

Baptism

Suffering and martyrdom were for the early Anabaptists a form of baptism. In the sixteenth century to embrace adult baptism was a deliberate break with the established church and a choice that placed one outside the accepted structures of the state. It entailed suffering and possible martyrdom. Anabaptists — as re-baptizers — understood well Paul's definition of baptism: "Do you not know that all of us who have been baptized into Christ Jesus were baptized into his death? Therefore we have been buried with him by baptism into death, so that, just as Christ was raised from the dead by the glory of the Father, so we too might walk in newness of life" (Romans 6:3–4). An early martyr, Hans Schlaffer (d. 1528), sang:

> Denn er sich hat durchs Wiederbad
> Ergeben bis gar in den Tod.
> [For the one who submits through rebaptism
> Submits even unto death.][13]

Rebaptism was then a blood baptism, as noted in 1 John 5:8: spirit, water, and blood. Another early hymn writer, Hans Betz, expressed the connection well:

Wer den Tauff nimmt, zu Hand ihm kommt
Kreuz, Trübsal und das Leiden.
[Whoever accepts the baptism immediately gets
Cross, trouble and suffering].[14]

Modern Anabaptists have long since lost the expectation of a baptism of blood, but the tradition remains. Baptism is indeed a dying to the luxuries and technology of this world, so the sense of "over against" remains.

Salvation

Although Anabaptists are fairly orthodox in their statements of faith, obviously some beliefs have been reinterpreted or differently understood. In the complex of ideas related to salvation, redemption, deliverance, and repentance, for example, each concept must be understood contextually. Salvation refers to a shift from the old age, which is passing away, to a new age which is visibly on the way. Jesus Christ has created the possibility of moving into that new age (salvation). While an Anabaptist might agree that Christ died for our sins, there is practically no Anabaptist allusion to a sacrificial death. Christ did suffer, but he did so more as a martyr than as a sacrificial lamb. There is practically no Anselmian sense of appeasement of the wrath of God. God is not an angry God, and people are not inherently evil. Insofar as the world is evil, it is passing away. Consequently, one seldom hears a sermon in which the pastor exhorts the listeners to repent, to be sorry for their sins, to acknowledge their guilt. There is little stress on personal salvation. According to legend, an Anabaptist who is asked, "Are you saved?" will respond, "From what?" A story is told of a Brethren elder, Rufus Bucher, who, returning from an evangelistic mission, was button-holed at the railroad station and asked, "Are you saved?" Bucher replied, "I like to think that I am. But you should go to my farm in Quarryville and ask my wife, my family, and my neighbors. I will accept their judgment on the matter."[15]

Theodicy

Suffering and ill health are seldom attached to wrongdoing or sin. Of course, Anabaptists are only human, and because they live in a society that attaches good fortune to piety and ill fortune to wrongdoing, in a particular moment of misfortune the believer might be tempted to ask, "What did I do wrong?" But, by and large, that is not the case. Consequently, Anabaptists do not ask why God caused them to suffer, to be in ill health, or to endure misfortune. Such things occur because we live in the conflict between two ages. God is not the cause of suffering and ill health. God (in Christ) is caught with us, and suffers with us, in the same end-time conflict. We may talk to God about our suffering, and we may even complain, but we cannot cast blame on God. The blame lies in the nature of the old age.

So when suffering and ill health come, the Anabaptist recognizes the present power of the old age. The Anabaptist has several solutions for the problem of suffering. The most obvious is to leave the old age behind and live as completely as possible in the community of the new age. Much suffering is caused by modern machinery and its emissions. Cancer is caused by the dumping of carcinogenic wastes. Psychological pollution is caused by television. This evil generation, which acts primarily for its own benefit rather than for the community of faith, causes suffering. So it is better to leave this age, to eschew modernization, to live simply away from the world. Every Anabaptist group has, at one time or another, chosen this route, and today Hutterites, and to some extent the Amish, still live in this belief system. Mennonites and Brethren have, for the most part, participated more in the old age, but they too reject the self-serving values of this age. Understanding that it is the conflict between the worldly kingdom and the kingdom of God that leads to suffering, Anabaptists do not ask why God has allowed these things; instead, they work for environmental improvement, fight the dumping of toxic wastes, call for healthful diets, live simply, develop community support systems, lobby in Washington for mutual improvement projects, and send agricultural assistance to underdeveloped areas.

Dying

O! wie ist die Zeit so wichtig,
Die uns Gott nur einmal giebt,
Und wie ist die welt so nichtig,
Die doch all-zu viel geliebt
Wird, dasz wir uns mit versäumen,
Geh'n da-hin so wie im Träumen,
Denkt so wenig an die Zeit
Der so langen Ewigkeit.
[Oh, how very important is the time,
Which God gives us only once,

And how worthless is the world
Which is loved so much,
That we lose ourselves,
Walking in the world as if in a dream,
Yet thinking so little about time
And what will last forever.]

— Alexander Mack, Sr. (1679–1735),
founder of the Church of the Brethren

In a communal context the understanding of death, like birth, stands in rather sharp contrast to death in more individualistic contexts. Life begins when a father and a mother want a child. The actual conception of that child occurs in an already existing structure and with pre-existing expectations. Without being too Skinnerian (or behavioristic), one must say that the formative elements of a child's life pre-exist.

Dying must be understood from the same perspective.[16] Everyone is a member of some community. Everyone has been formed by and, in turn, helped form his or her community. When biological life terminates, the individual does not leave community, but that relationship does indeed change. Resurrection-existence (my term for community existence after death) normally takes on a positive note, as the community remembers the useful contribution of the individual who has "died." The individual is aware, perhaps unconsciously, of such a future community existence. While death has a painful finality to it, the community member anticipates resurrection-existence. Indeed, the resurrection-existence will often start to take shape before biological death.

Surely one aspect of martyrdom is the certainty of resurrection-existence. The martyr knows that the faith community has *already* purified her or his memory so that the individual can die with the knowledge that resurrection has occurred. Preservation of present life or hope for continued individual existence (immortality) seems less important than resurrection within the faith community. *Martyrs' Mirror* and the Hutterian *Chronicle* primarily contain stories that assure the martyr of resurrection-existence in the faith community. The stories were undoubtedly written to communicate the purity of anticipated resurrection-existence; one gathers from them a somewhat idealized view, as the faithful exhibit more theological acumen, more biblical knowledge, more courage before their persecutors, and more exemplary qualities than one would have expected in ordinary life.

The meaning of dying in the Anabaptist context cannot properly be understood without knowing the anthropology that produces it. As indicated earlier, Anabaptism belongs to a low individualism–high community type of social organization. The boundary of the individual is weak. In fact, the term *body* refers as much to the boundary of the community as it does to the boundary of the individual. The person is formed in the "body" and eventually becomes conscious of herself or himself as a person within the body. But the value system, the ethics, the reaction characteristics have been formed by the communal body. The person seldom rejects these ingrained, often unconsciously grasped qualities. Indeed, if the individual has to think about it or justify community qualities, it is highly likely that he or she has also lost the sense of body. Decision making results much more from peer direction and the willingness to live according to community direction (called *Gelassenheit* in the Mennonite tradition). As in the biblical community, the heart (will) is much more important than the mind (reason).

In communitarian anthropology there is no certainty of objectivity nor relativity of subjectivity. Reality lies in dyadic relationships. When subject cannot separate from object, then all relationships will be empathic; that is, an individual is never certain whether what is happening to another person is not also happening to him or her. Such empathy is necessary, of course, for mutual community. In community the distinction between the individual and the corporate will always be difficult to see. The relationship is what many of us would call "corporate personality." The individual does not exist as one in a series of persons living in a common place (an Aristotelian perspective). Nor does the individual exist as a shadow or type of the corporate entity, a Platonic concept. Rather, every individual represents the total community. Or, to put it another way, the one and the many are the same.

Communities with Resurrection-Existence Life

The presence of martyrs among early Anabaptists created communities preeminently conscious of death. Because death could come at any time, the entire community lived with a sense of life after death, that is, resurrection-existence. When a community lives in a resurrection-existence state, the values of this world pass away. Persons do not relate to each other in terms of wealth, success, position, education, or power. Communities of resurrection-life become genuine societies of honor and shame. All that really matters is that resurrection (everlasting honor) occur and that present existence be a foretaste of one's life after death. Anabaptist retirement homes can be such communities.

There are many reasons why modern society has created homes for the elderly — chief among them are the difficulties of maintaining an extended family in a more mobile society, forced retirement, longer life expectancy, and the cost of care for the elderly.[17] But Mennonites and Brethren — more aware, perhaps, of communities of resurrection-existence — have spent considerable energy, effort, and resources to build homes where honor can be attained and mutual caring can be found.

Older persons may well lament the loss of extended family, and, with some justification, seek to restore it. Yet if life progresses in stages, then peers are as important, if not more so, than families. The child is born in a natural family but eventually shifts from natural family to secondary family (the church body, for example). As life continues, other types of community can and should emerge. For the elderly the constant presence of terminal illness and death itself creates yet a different kind of peer relationship.

Although we are born (die to the womb) into a natural family, it is continuing death that creates secondary families. The Anabaptist act of baptism signifies our death to the natural family and our anticipated inclusion in a new family. In the end stages of life, death takes on a new meaning. Death represents more than the end of past stages of life, loss of past relationships, displacement from past spaces.[18] The new life after death is what we are calling the resurrection-existence life. A community of the resurrection will be marked by the following:

1. A presence in one's prior communities that continues prior dyadic (one-on-one) relationships.

2. A satisfactory (purified) quality of relationship with previous communities. Paul calls it incorruptibility (2 Corinthians 4:16–5:5), but we can think of the new life as one without shame.

3. A peer trust based on death rather than life. Such a trust does not expect accomplishments or rewards; instead, one expects that people will walk with each other to the edge of life.

In communities of resurrection-life, authority over the process of life should be left in the hands of those who share key dyadic relationships. Because a person who lives in the death covenant no longer measures life by achievement, rewards, and longevity, it is critical that the last stages of life be carried out with honor in the eyes of significant peers. The person

who enters the last stages of life should be understood as one who is living out of the resurrection. It is inappropriate to take such a person from
the context of peer relationships in order to save his or her biological life.
Because nothing is more important at this point than the resurrection, decisions regarding medical procedures should not be made by administrators
and medical personnel. Family and peers should decide what is honorable,
and, with or without prior consent of the patient, the instructions of this
support group should be legally mandatory.

While it is true that the elderly have "died" to previous communities
and have been resurrected (made incorruptible), it is essential that members of the community of resurrection-existence share their faith with
others. Such communities of retired persons are a continuous counterculture; that is, they have learned to live outside our cultural value system. As
much as possible, retirement communities should be located where retired
persons can express their value system, share their experiences, and utilize their resurrection-existence skills. The placement of such communities
in idyllic, pastoral settings misses the point of life defined by developing
stages. One of the resurrection-existence skills is the ability to form in-
tergenerational and intercapability dyads. Most obvious are relationships
between the elderly and the chronically ill, or the permanently disadvantaged. By caring for others in need the elderly can make a parabolic
witness to mutual caring and at the same time be of considerable value to
those disadvantaged.

Anabaptist Retirement Homes

Hutterites have not developed retirement homes because they still provide care in extended families. Among the Hutterites an older person is
never excluded from the function of the community, but at a certain point
older persons are gently shifted from responsible tasks to honorable positions.[19] Mennonites and Brethren followed the same pattern until the
late nineteenth century. The first Mennonite retirement homes were built
between 1894 and 1899. Among Mennonites in Canada and the United
States there are now more than one hundred retirement homes (compared
to twelve in 1940). Between 1883 and 1910 the Brethren groups built thirteen retirement homes. At the present time the Church of the Brethren
itself has twenty-five.[20]

Not all Anabaptist retirement homes are the same or of equal quality, but by and large they show the same caring values. Some, like Green-croft in Goshen, Indiana, and Timbercrest in North Manchester, Indiana, are almost national models for retirement homes. Anabaptist homes normally are built near some educational institution or denominational center. They are seldom near large cities, but they usually provide some opportunity for continuing education, for volunteer service, and intercapability relationships. The so-called campus will consist of free-standing homes or independent living units (for retired persons who need little care), resident health care apartments (for persons who need some assistance), and health care units (for persons who need constant attention). When persons enter the retirement village, it is understood that their initial payment will carry them through whatever level of care they need. While the denominations do not directly support retirement homes, it is inconceivable that someone would be asked to leave because his or her funds were exhausted.

In 1988–89 a new organization was formed that combined the various associations of Mennonite and Brethren homes. The Association for Brethren and Mennonite Ministries with Older Adults pulls together organizations and homes with a common Anabaptist direction. It could not only have far-reaching implications for ministry to older adults but also serve as a model for cooperation at other levels of health ministry.

Hospices

Hospices for the terminally ill were first developed in 1960 by Dr. Cicely Saunders of St. Christopher's Hospice in London. Since then the hospice movement has spread rapidly in the United States and Canada (where it is called palliative care). Generally speaking, hospices follow the philosophy that death is a natural stage in the life span. In a home (hospice) set aside for terminal patients, teams of physicians, nurses, counselors, and volunteers work with the family to attain what we have called resurrection-life. No hospices have been built by Anabaptist groups, but large numbers of Brethren and Mennonites work in hospices as health care providers or volunteers. Although governmental agencies and health insurance companies have been slow in supporting hospices, this type of care obviously fits well with the Anabaptist understanding of dying.

Dying is a community matter. The one who dies belongs to the community, and the community takes form in the one who dies (the many are one).

To take the individual away from the community (into intensive care, for example) *before* resurrection-existence has been realized does damage to family, community, and individual — damage that can *never* be repaired (in community formation matters, Anabaptists tend to consider process irreversible). And if resurrection-existence has *already* been realized, attempts to save the biological life can only disturb the life of the community: to attempt to recoup a prior stage by heroic measures will only obfuscate the life of the individual in resurrection-existence. Neither community nor individual would want that.

Death Rituals

For the most part Anabaptists have buried their dead with simplicity and solemnity. Because the deceased had not really left the community, excessive displays of grief were not common. The Church of the Brethren did not even allow benedictions until late in the nineteenth century.

News of death moves rapidly in a close community. Within two days nearly all relatives and friends have been notified (often by networking). Among the Hutterites the other colonies are informed by telephone. As many as possible gather for the funeral. It is important to pay respects to the deceased, but perhaps even more important to share in the deceased's resurrection-life and to be a part of the community as it reconstitutes itself without the physical presence of the deceased. For some, to miss these moments would be unthinkable.

Customs differ from place to place and group to group, but this description of a Hutterite funeral would ring true for most Anabaptists:

> The funeral of Michael Decker on June 30, 1973, was larger than most. As steward of the Tschetter Colony in South Dakota, he had been well known in all the colonies in South Dakota and Canada. The service was to be held in the dining hall, because it accommodated more people than the schoolhouse. The pallbearers, who were nephews of the deceased, carried the casket from the home to the service at three o'clock in the afternoon. Some of the older persons had already gathered together when the casket was brought in and placed in the center of the large dining area, encircled by chairs for the close relatives. The full-length lid of the coffin was removed for the service. Seated at the head of the coffin were all the preachers; the women and men sat separately on rows of benches on either side of the deceased. The one-hour service began and ended with a hymn led by the oldest preacher. The sermon, read by one of the several elders present, took the frailty of life as a predominating theme.

After completing the sermon, the preacher sat down briefly. He then arose and in a few short words committed the body to the earth for burial. All who wished could take a last view of the deceased by rising to their feet. No line was formed to walk past the coffin. After the mourners had left the room, the casket was placed on a truck, which the procession followed to the colony cemetery on a nearby hill. Without ceremony the body was lowered into an open grave and immediately covered with earth. When the earth formed a slight mound all of the men removed their hats. The preacher issued a short statement of thanks in behalf of the bereaved family. The burial was complete.[21]

Like many cultures the Anabaptist tradition features a common meal as an essential part of the death rites. The Hutterites prepare considerable food, including the traditional funeral buns. The meal is of course a courtesy for the family of the deceased, especially for those who have traveled a long distance, but it is more important as a moment for the family to establish the resurrection-life and to develop a new family structure. At the meal the grieving stops, and stories shift from reactions to the news about the death to stories of happy days with the deceased. Laughter ensues. The family remakes itself anew in the image of the old; for example, if the deceased was a great-grandmother, then one of her daughters steps forward as the new *mater familias*. Relatives and friends leave knowing that the deceased now lives in resurrection-existence, already purified in the family tradition; knowing that the family will go on with a new structure which includes the old; and knowing that when they die it will be the same. The meal marks this important transition.

The resurrection or what we call resurrection-existence does not depend on a physical body but on one's continued existence in the faith community. Consequently the preservation of the physical body has little importance for Anabaptists. Destruction of the bodies of the early Anabaptist martyrs, as for the early Christians, had little deterrent value. The physical body was not ultimate, though the body of Christ was. Anabaptists, therefore, have no difficulty with organ donations from the deceased. Indeed, most Anabaptist wellness groups call for the use of a living will that would allow for the transplanting of the deceased's organs and advance directives for termination of biological life without heroic measures.

Because preserving the body has little meaning, Anabaptists lean toward simplicity in regard to burial itself.[22] Anabaptists often participate in local efforts to legalize and make available inexpensive burials. If simplicity and expenses are a concern, and if the body has no particular value, one might suppose cremation would be more common, yet Anabaptists, for the most part, do not practice cremation. This is probably due in part to the necessity to have a body present when the community enters into resurrection-existence with the deceased. In theory the community could celebrate resurrection-existence with ashes, but psychologically it has not proven satisfactory. The presence of a lifeless body signifies death and separation more powerfully than would ashes.

·7·

The Vision Revisited

In 1939 something important happened to the Anabaptist movement. That mutual love which had been directed inward shifted to a compassion for the world; the sense of community was radically expanded; and rural parochialism gave way to global action. We have seen this alteration in the kinds of projects preferred by Anabaptists, and we have seen major modifications in the way Anabaptists think (responsibility in discipleship and mutuality in love). As Anabaptists face the implications of this radical alteration they will need continually to reconsider the vision. It was the Mennonite leader Harold Bender who restated the Anabaptist vision following the 1939 paradigm shift. He spoke of three key elements: discipleship; the church as a voluntary, separated fellowship; and the priority of love and nonresistance in all relationships.[1] The Anabaptist vision has preserved an important element of the Christian heritage. While it ought not be protected as a minority voice, neither should it be lost in some ecclesiastical museum.

When Anabaptists come to a key point in their life, they read the Bible. The questions asked of the Bible by Anabaptists today differ considerably from those asked by Menno Simons, Jacob Hut, Peter Rideman, Alexander Mack, and Harold Bender. In every generation the readaptation of the vision will depend in large part on a rereading of the Bible, especially the New Testament. Rereading the New Testament is a corporate task, yet occasionally some persons can sense the hermeneutical direction of the community and can advance proposals concerning the Anabaptist future.

So in this chapter let us look again at the New Testament and, in light of the traditional vision and practice of the Anabaptists, look at future directions in health care.

Communitarians interpret the Bible in ways that are not readily understood in more mainline churches or in academia. Anabaptists are a community of interpretation gathered around the New Testament, which is itself a community of interpretation around the Jesus tradition. Anabaptist scholars argue that this hermeneutical stance allows the present community of faith to read the text in a way it was intended — as a document of the community. Aware of this difference, contemporary Anabaptists have planned a series of commentaries on the Bible from a Believers' Church perspective. The foreword to the series states:

> Believers church people have always been known for their emphasis on obedience to the simple meaning of the Scripture. Because of this, they do not have a long history of deep historical-critical biblical scholarship. [A Believers' Church commentary] series attempts to be faithful to the Scriptures while also taking archaeology and current biblical studies seriously. Doing this means that at many points the writers will not differ greatly from the interpretations which can be found in many other good commentaries. Yet basic presuppositions about Christ, the church and its mission, God and history, human nature, the Christian life, and other doctrines do shape a writer's interpretation of Scripture. Thus this series, like all other commentaries, stands within a specific historical church tradition.[2]

Such an Anabaptist reading of the New Testament would include reading (1) to understand the formation and maintenance of community; (2) to understand the relationship of revelation to social matrix; (3) to understand the faith of the mass of believers rather than the few who are writers; (4) to understand the locus of ultimate authority; and (5) to understand the driving force of the new faith.[3]

Put in more traditional terms, Anabaptists consider Jesus central to their faith.[4] They look to the early church around Jesus as a community that should be studied and emulated. They see the formation of the state church under Constantine as the fall of this early community of faith (*Gemeinschaft*).[5] With these concerns in mind we take a new look at the biblical vision.

Jesus before Culture

While most of the New Testament authors normally castigate those who do not understand the gospel as they have presented it (for example, Mark 4:11–12; 8:33; 9:18–19; 1 Corinthians 2:14), there are a few instances where they protect or even praise those who have not necessarily understood.

In John 20:29, for example, Jesus said to Thomas, "Have you believed because you have seen me? Blessed are those who have not seen and yet have come to believe." In the Gospel of John the term for appropriate perception is "to see." In the call of the disciples the four are invited to "come and see" (1:39, 46). In that paradigmatic statement of conversion the man born blind can see and then confess Jesus as Lord and Son of Man (9:37–39). Indeed, Jesus acknowledges the man's conversion by saying "you have *seen* him [the Son of man]" (v. 37). At the end of the original Gospel, Thomas missed the first meeting of the disciples where they claimed to have "seen" the Lord (20:20, 25). Thomas does manage to make the second meeting where he too sees Jesus. John's Jesus ends the narrative with the rather incredible statement: "Blessed are those who have *not seen* and yet have come to believe." Given the interior logic of the Gospel of John, it must have been the narrator's blessing on those of the early church who participate but have not yet been able to "see."

In Matthew 25:31–46 we find a similar statement:

> "When the Son of Man comes in his glory, and all the angels with him, then he will sit on the throne of his glory. All the nations will be gathered before him, and he will separate people one from another as a shepherd separates the sheep from the goats, and he will put the sheep at his right hand and the goats at the left. Then the king will say to those at his right hand, 'Come, you that are blessed by my Father, inherit the kingdom prepared for you from the foundation of the world; for I was hungry and you gave me food, I was thirsty and you gave me something to drink, I was a stranger and you welcomed me, I was naked and you gave me clothing, I was sick and you took care of me, I was in prison and you visited me.' Then the righteous will answer him, 'Lord, when was it that we saw you hungry and gave you food, or thirsty and gave you something to drink? And when was it that we saw you a stranger and welcomed you, or naked and gave you clothing? And when was it that we saw you sick or in prison and visited you?' And the king will answer them, 'Truly I tell you, just as you did it to one of the least of these who are members of my family, you did it to me.' Then he will say to those at his left hand, 'You that are accursed, depart from me into the eternal fire prepared for the devil and his angels; for I was hungry and you gave me no food, I was thirsty and you gave me nothing to drink, I was a stranger and you did not welcome me, naked and you did not give me clothing, sick and in prison and you did not visit me.' Then they also will answer, 'Lord, when was it that we saw you hungry or thirsty or a stranger or naked or sick or in prison, and did not take care of you?' Then he will answer them, 'Truly I tell you, just as you did not do it to one of the least of these, you did not do it to me.' And these will go away into eternal punishment, but the righteous into eternal life."

In the Gospel of Matthew, "the least of these" (*mikroi*) are those who do not exhibit qualities of leadership or exhibit any power within the faith community. Such qualities of leadership are presumably held by the apostles and disciples. But in the so-called parable of the Last Judgment, Jesus praises those who feed, offer hospitality to, clothe, and visit the little ones. Those who did such things were unaware of what they had done. They acted with compassion out of their own community formation, not out of ethical reflection or even intentional obedience. They were "spontaneous Christians" and are praised for that. Presumably they, too, belong to the community of the little people, the unreflective members of the faith community.

Paul, who often chastises his readers for lack of understanding, also has empathy for those who may be bewildered by the intricacies of his teaching. In 1 Corinthians 3:1–3 he writes, "And so, brothers and sisters, I could not speak to you as spiritual people, but rather as people of the flesh, as infants in Christ. I fed you with milk, not solid food, for you were not ready for solid food. Even now you are still not ready, for you are still of the flesh. For as long as there is jealousy and quarreling among you, are you not of the flesh, and behaving according to human inclinations?" Paul wished to address his readers as persons of the spirit (*pneumatikoi*), but they simply were not at that stage of development. Meanwhile, since they are still infants he must address them as persons of the flesh (*sarkikoi*). The conflict at Corinth in itself proves that they are not ready for the solid food of adult adherents. Perhaps the same group comprises the weak of 8:7–13. While Paul may lament the weakness of some new converts, he does not excoriate them for their lack of perception. Rather he insists that the strong must not cause the weak to stumble.

Church historian Ramsay MacMullen has insisted that only a few of the new converts to Christianity during the first three centuries came from those intellectuals or leaders who might have given to us the literature of early Christianity.[6] He rightly asks how the vast majority of early Christians made the shift from paganism to Christianity and under what circumstances that conversion occurred. New Testament passages such as these reflect a situation that was quite common in later centuries — there were persons who were Christian but who could not articulate a minimally coherent faith.

MacMullen understands the problem well, but he deals primarily with a Christianity that had already become a culture (fourth century). We need to ask if we can trace popular conversion *prior* to the appearance of the

Christian culture. During the first three centuries of church history, how did the majority of believers become Christians? One would assume that some alteration occurred in the believers' social matrix, an alteration that made them Christian. If this is correct, we need to determine the common elements of a social matrix and ask how the Jesus tradition might have altered them.

Recent efforts to analyze, from a sociological perspective, the relationship of a faith to a culture find a constant dialectical relationship between the power of the faith and the form of the culture.[7] The life of a social matrix (Little Community) normally follows a certain grid, but in actuality it also interacts with a religious and ethical tradition (Great Tradition).[8] Characteristics of any social matrix will be (1) a cohesive extended family; (2) a strong sense of local community; (3) a strong, authoritative leadership; (4) a strong tradition for the celebration of natural, communal, and personal events; and (5) a close relationship to nature or land. According to such studies a religious faith can influence and alter these elements of the social matrix but cannot eliminate them. Likewise the social matrix may influence and alter the religious faith, but it cannot make a social matrix of it.[9] For example, some gnostics (early Christians who practiced intense spirituality) attempted to disparage the family, and some attempted to separate the religious actor from this material world. Such forms of gnosticism have long since disappeared in favor of the needs of the social matrix.

Is there any way to determine the original impulse of Christianity in regard to the social matrix? Was our New Testament canon not formed for use within a specific culture (the Greco-Roman)? Can we find that faith which existed before the canon was formed?

South African scholar Itumeleng Mosala has proposed that the present New Testament was formed by Christian communities at a time when it had already adapted to a "middle-class" virtue system.[10] To retrieve the New Testament for the oppressed, he proposed using the tools of biblical criticism to discover a New Testament that existed earlier than our present canon. When students from other cultures, for example, reflect on this proposal, they often say that Jesus was a Jew, but Jesus Christ (the resurrected Lord) belongs *sui generis* to their culture. Sometimes, but not always, they can demonstrate their point with art: Jesus has been portrayed as a Jew, but the resurrection stories show Jesus the Christ as Taiwanese, Japanese, Korean, or African. Their distinction between Jesus and Jesus the Christ certainly marks a frequently used, possible point of departure. That is,

Jesus was historical, but faith in Jesus must be extrahistorical (historical, but more than historical). That which is historical belongs to a certain culture at a certain time (the Jews as a Little Community), but that which is extrahistorical belongs to whatever culture in which it becomes effective (the Great Tradition).

What is that Christianity which stands in dialectical tension with any social matrix? What is it in the Jesus tradition that calls forth the faith community? If we assume that the canon of the New Testament is a cultural adaptation, then the Jesus tradition must be the original Christian "Great Tradition." With some degree of assurance the Jesus tradition can be ascertained. While one would not claim to know Jesus' very words or actions, one can monitor the process by which the tradition became acculturated. Within certain limitations the scholar can reverse that process in such a way that the original Jesus tradition can be determined.

New Testament scholar Dominic Crossan has recently attempted to establish the primary levels of the Jesus tradition by sorting the Gospel material into various chronological levels and noting how often a story or saying appears in the earliest levels. Using this test of chronological multiple attestation (the number of times a story appears in the earliest traditions), what can we learn about the Jesus tradition and the Palestinian social matrix?

Family Cohesion

The Jesus tradition comes to us with a mixed message. The statement on marriage and divorce is one of the best-attested sayings of Jesus: "To the married I give this command — not I but the Lord — that the wife should not separate from her husband (but if she does separate, let her remain unmarried or else be reconciled to her husband), and that the husband should not divorce his wife" (1 Corinthians 7:10–11).[11] In contrast with contemporary Jewish custom, the earliest Jesus tradition did not countenance divorce. At its earliest (prior to 55 C.E.?) level the traditional prohibition against divorce probably reflected a sexual reality (the two shall become one flesh) more than a legal demand for the new community. But before the turn of the century the form of the saying used in Q (the earliest sayings source used by Matthew and Luke) was already used as a legal guide to allow divorce in the case of fornication (Matthew 5:31–32).

On the other hand, there are significant sayings about hating one's family. Jesus said, "Whoever does not hate father and mother cannot be my disciple, and whoever does not hate brothers and sisters, and carry the cross as I do, will not be worthy of me."[12] In a similar way we hear of the true family of Jesus: "The disciples said to him, 'Your brothers and your mother are standing outside.' He said to them, 'Those here who do what my Father wants are my brothers and are my mother. They are the ones who will enter my Father's domain.' "[13]

Over against Judaism the Jesus tradition stressed the unity of the family, but at the same time it called for a strong end-time individuation that transferred family loyalty to the end-time community of faith.[14]

Community

One can see early Jesus traditions, such as healing, used by the later church to stress the forgiveness of sin:

> When he returned to Capernaum after some days, it was reported that he was at home. So many gathered around that there was no longer room for them, not even in front of the door; and he was speaking the word to them. Then some people came, bringing to him a paralyzed man, carried by four of them. And when they could not bring him to Jesus because of the crowd, they removed the roof above him; and after having dug through it, they let down the mat on which the paralytic lay. When Jesus saw their faith, *he said to the paralytic, "Son, your sins are forgiven." Now some of the scribes were sitting there, questioning in their hearts, "Why does this fellow speak in this way? It is blasphemy! Who can forgive sins but God alone?" At once Jesus perceived in his spirit that they were discussing these questions among themselves; and he said to them, "Why do you raise such questions in your hearts? Which is easier, to say to the paralytic, 'Your sins are forgiven,' or to say, 'Stand up and take your mat and walk'? But so that you may know that the Son of Man has authority on earth to forgive sins"* — he said to the paralytic — "I say to you, stand up, take your mat and go to your home." And he stood up, and immediately took the mat and went out before all of them; so that they were all amazed and glorified God, saying, "We have never seen anything like this!" (Mark 2:1–12; emphasis added)

Into this story of the healing of the paralytic the story of the forgiveness of sin has been inserted (vv. 5b–10). While both stories may well have been a part of the original oral tradition, the church wanted to attach the theological teaching on forgiveness to the formation of community (healing of the unclean).

It would seem probable that in the original Jesus tradition Jesus obliterated the distinction between clean and unclean. By healing and casting out demons he broke those boundaries that the social matrix had erected. Indeed, he reestablished total human community in a way that stood in tension with the temple and normative systems.

Jesus not only obliterated boundaries but also ate with all levels of society. He instructed his twelve disciples to eat with all and to heal the sick (Mark 6:6b–13):

> Then he went about among the villages teaching. He called the twelve and began to send them out two by two, and gave them authority over the unclean spirits. He ordered them to take nothing for their journey except a staff; no bread, no bag, no money in their belts; but to wear sandals and not to put on two tunics. He said to them, "Wherever you enter a house, stay there until you leave the place. If any place will not welcome you and they refuse to hear you, as you leave, shake off the dust that is on your feet as a testimony against them." So they went out and proclaimed that all should repent. They cast out many demons, and anointed with oil many who were sick and cured them.

The spread of the new faith depended on the development of a universal community and the destruction of class or other artificial distinctions. The universality of the actions and message of Jesus placed the new faith in tension with the Jewish social matrix and maintained itself by means of a powerful vision of the future.

Jesus instructed his disciples to build community by developing habits of mutuality. In the "sending" passages (which occur early and frequently and are thus considered to be highly attested parts of the Jesus tradition), disciples and missioners are advised to go from place to place accepting and giving mutual support.[15] The equally attested saying about "seeking" urges the disciples to ask for what they want because (in mutuality) it will be granted: "let them that seek not stop seeking until they find. When they find, they will be disturbed. When they are disturbed, they will marvel, and will reign over all" (Gospel of Thomas 2). And when mutuality occurs, it will prove to be revolutionary! Another primary example of sharing with the community, the feeding of the five thousand, also comes from early multiple attestation.

Accounts of Jesus healing the sick and eating with others occur early and often.[16] One could conclude that the Jesus tradition at its earliest level consisted of (1) healings of persons regardless of their status as clean or unclean; (2) universal commensalism regardless of class distinctions; (3) development of community through mutuality; (4) a constant tension with the social matrix (as seen in Jesus' crucifixion by the social matrix and in his constant use of apocalyptic reversal, for example, the Beatitudes); and (5) subversion of political limitations (as seen in his sending of the disciples to create inclusivity and in his apocalyptic vision of a universal community).

Authority

As indicated in the discussion of community, the over-against nature of the Jesus tradition placed the first believers in conflict with accepted authorities. While on the one hand the descent of Jesus from the line of David was affirmed early and often,[17] the Jesus tradition broke clearly with prescribed authorities on such matters as dietary laws (concerning clean and unclean),[18] means of forgiving sins,[19] the authority of Scripture,[20] and the power of the temple.[21] The apocalyptic nature of the Jesus tradition[22] kept the emerging faith community in tension with the old age and the authorities of the old age (1 Corinthians 6:1-6).

Life Celebrations

Though many of the parables speak of feasts, weddings, and other celebrations, there is little in the early Jesus tradition regarding the significance of life celebrations and annual ceremonies. Even the Sabbath controversies lack major attestation in the earliest traditions. More to the point, perhaps, is the early Eucharist tradition[23] that reflects the Passover celebration. Basically the earliest Jesus tradition offers no celebrative events except for the resignification of the Passover meal as a deliverance event.

The Land

Most of the New Testament shows little interest in the land. The end-time vision of Christianity points toward a city (Hebrews 13:14; Revelation 21:2). Jesus does tell many parables involving the land, and the land in some parables was taken by some early Christians as a reference to Israel (Mark 12:1-12). Otherwise the Jesus tradition gives no value to the land. To be sure there are narratives that indicate Jesus was attached to the land, such as that of the Syrophoenician woman (Mark 7:24–30) or the Gerasene demoniac (Mark 5:1–20), but these are not necessarily from the earliest tradition.

Popular Christianity before Constantine

As I indicated in the beginning, there is within the New Testament itself a concern for those persons converted to Christianity who do not necessarily share the faith perspective of the author or editor. Furthermore, one can see in the New Testament the continuing adaptation of the precultural Jesus tradition to the social matrix. Such adaptation occurred in the interest of "mass" conversion. For example, Paul's message is adapted to the social matrix by means of the Pastoral Epistles, and John's message is adapted by means of the Johannine Epistles.[24] One can see in these adaptations the assimilation of the religious faith by the social matrix.

Another method of assessing the nature of early folk Christianity is to examine Christian culture when it did finally appear. About 180 C.E. several symbols appeared which, because of the context, have to be understood as Christian. Shortly afterward pictures appeared that either utilized those symbols or should be understood as references to biblical narratives.

In terms of artistic symbols, the first Christian culture used the lamb, anchor, vase, dove, boat, olive branch, praying figure (*orante*), palm, bread, good shepherd, fish, and a vine and grapes.[25] All these independent symbols had a pre-Christian history. The first Christians did not offer substitute symbols (early Christianity had none), but so utilized these that later they came to represent the nascent Christian faith. One might say these Greco-Roman symbols were "infected" by a Christian virus and in that way altered. The precultural Jesus traditions we have noted were significantly present in these first sets of symbols. Healing was expressed by the community peace symbols: the dove and the olive branch (and eventually the *orante*). Tension with the dominant culture was expressed by the boat, the anchor, and likely the fish (if we assume that water symbolized the dominant social matrix). Mutuality is expressed by that powerful, frequent symbol of the early church, the good shepherd; in context it represents the hospitality offered by the community to individuals apparently alienated by the dominant culture. And the hope for good life was expressed by the tree. When the symbols became pictorial,[26] especially as related to biblical stories, nearly all the Old Testament pictures portrayed an *orante* caught in a difficult situation, yet delivered by a person of God or a divine act. One thinks of Noah and the ark, Moses and the rock, Daniel between two lions, three young men in the fiery furnace, and Susanna and the elders as images of divine deliverance from difficult political or social situations. The popular representation of Jonah and the sea monster probably stressed mission toward the alien social matrix. In New Testament pictorial episodes there is more emphasis on healing itself: one finds the healing of the paralytic, the resurrection of Lazarus, and the healing of a blind boy.

Commensalism is expressed by frequent portrayals of the Eucharist (bread, fish, and wine) as well as frequent portrayals of an *agape* meal: baskets of loaves (seven or twelve), fish, and wine — much like the feeding of the five thousand). In most cases the agape meal has been expanded to include the significant dead. For example, one early meal shows the honored guest in a pose precisely like Endymion, a dead hero on Roman sarcophagi.[27]

There is little in early Christian art to indicate the locus of authority. The formation of the so-called Crypt of the Popes in St. Callistus may be the first (about 250 C.E.) archaeological evidence for an authority issue. Apparently the graves of the Roman hierarchy had replaced the graves of the martyrs and saints. In regard to land, only the paradisaical Orpheus scenes with its tree would indicate the urban yearning for land.[28]

Judging by early Christian popular art, we can say that celebration of life events and the cycle of nature increased dramatically in the faith community. We have already noted the celebration of the Eucharist and the agape meal, particularly as associated with the meal for the dead. In contrast to the Jesus tradition, baptism also plays a central role. The earliest art portrays the young man Jesus being baptized by an old man (river God), with a dove descending from above. In regard to natural cycles, apparently both Judaism and Christianity fought the social matrix over the winter solstice. The nearly universal celebration of the winter solstice eventually forced Christianity to adapt traditions around, and a date for, the birth of Jesus as a means of displacing competitive religious systems (in this case the birth of the sun god). The first intimations of such a struggle can be found in the only certain pre-Constantinian mosaic — the beautiful portrayal of Christ crossing the sky as Apollo — in mausoleum M under St. Peter's. Probably the contemporary emphasis on the ascension of Elijah was another attempt to displace the pervasive sun chariot.[29]

At first, at least, the early church did universalize its community. Not only was family extended, but delimiting boundaries were consistently broken. In that sense Christianity continued an end-time pressure on the social matrix. For example, Roman slaves who had been freed were usually buried with the name of their prior owner attached to their slave name, and in that way we know they once had been slaves. When the Christian culture appeared and Christian graves could be identified, there was no mention of prior slavery.[30] The amazing growth of the Christian community during this period must have been a product of the original Jesus tradition.

We can summarize the effect of the Jesus tradition on the faith community prior to Constantine as follows:

Family. The Jesus tradition speaks of the family as indissoluble, yet it subordinates the family to the faith community. The popular church stresses the faith community as family.

Community. Jesus called for universal community and created it by healings that obviated the distinction between clean and unclean and by eating with persons of all social levels. The popular church also stressed healing across social boundaries and created community by eating together.

Authority. Jesus stood over against Jewish and Roman authorities and offered leadership roles to those who served. The popular church resisted the social matrix and registered continued conflict with the state. There is little reflection on authority within the faith community.

Life celebrations. Jesus said little about the passage of life. The popular church celebrated formal meals, baptism, death, and anniversaries of death dates. The church also struggled with the calendar of the social matrix.

Land. Except for the analogous use of land, Jesus did not deal with the meaning of land in general or even the Land in particular. This issue did not generate much concern in popular Christianity before Constantine.

The Greco-Roman Canon

Christianity took on a particular cultural form based on a symbol system rooted in the Greco-Roman tradition. Much of that earliest Christian culture was true to the original precultural Jesus tradition. But such a development was not historically necessary. The earliest Jesus tradition could have moved more universally into Egypt and Africa. Then Europe would have been "invaded" by an African cultural Christianity. Is it possible to repeat the assimilation process in other cultures without going through the Greco-Roman original? The Jesus tradition could attach to any other culture and a Christianity be produced that had none of the Greco-Roman characteristics. Indeed, in the early centuries the Christian faith did enter cultures that were not classified as Greco-Roman, and such cultures do differ from the Roman adaptation. One thinks particularly of the Phrygian, Syriac, and Celtic.

The canon of the Roman church ought not be jettisoned. It indicates how the variety of faith expressions can be united under one catholic church. If there is to be a large number of disparate Christian cultures, the canon will be a necessary guide to the formation of a universal community. Furthermore, the canon demonstrates how the precultural faith had related to one specific culture — the Greco-Roman. Christians of a non–Greco-Roman culture have every right to seek the precultural Jesus tradition and its early community, and to use that as a guide for their own culture. That precultural Jesus tradition will stand in dialectical relationship to any new social matrix. It cannot be totally assimilated by any other culture without destroying the Jesus tradition itself.

There is a Jesus tradition that touches any social matrix, but it is not wedded to the Greco-Roman. When it touches the social matrix it forms a close community with universal dimensions. When it becomes standardized, as it did under Constantine, it loses its power to create *Gemeinschaft*. When the *koinonia*, the community, was lost, conversion of the ordinary folk occurred by means of force and persuasion.

Anabaptists are a New Testament church with a strong Jesus orientation. At critical times of decision making Anabaptists turn again and again to the New Testament for guidance and inspiration. They do understand that their own situation has changed through the centuries and that their interpretation of the New Testament should change accordingly. This is such a time of change. As Anabaptists wrestle more and more with the formation of global communities, the question of Jesus becomes increasingly critical. Do we have a Jesus to offer who is not bound by Western customs, symbols, and regulations? As we have seen, New Testament scholarship does offer the possibility of knowing a Jesus tradition that precedes our Western canon. With such a Jesus as guide, Anabaptists can look forward to new directions in global health ministry.

Vision for the Next Century: Base Communities

shared bread is the experience of people as community,
and therefore the experience of god.
it is communion at once human and divine.
it is so all over the world,
it has been so all through the ages.
a central concern of jesus is to promote table fellowship
and get people to share bread and life.

. . . .

shared food is concerted action to build community.
community has its necessary material basis in community of wealth,
in the common possession of the one earth.
the cup we bless is a sharing in the outpoured life of jesus.
and the bread we break is a sharing in the given body of jesus.
"because the loaf of bread is one,
we, many though we are, are one body,
for we all partake of the one body."
if then in the church one goes hungry while another is sated and drunk, the
    reality of the church is violated,
and what is eaten is no longer the supper of the lord.
without the fraternity founded on shared food and community of resources,
there is neither church nor its celebration in the eucharist.
"therefore, my brothers, when you assemble for the meal,
    wait for one another."

—Samuel Rayan,
"Give Us This Day Our Daily Bread"

Given the Anabaptist tradition, the present world situation, and the New Testament vision, the Anabaptist health agenda for the next century becomes clear. The tradition has been communitarian; since World War II that communitarian tradition has been globalized. The Jesus tradition calls for breaking down of boundaries; for building of local communities among the disenfranchised; for challenging the social matrix. Jesus did this by healing both clean and unclean, by eating together with all, and by facing anyone who objected to his vision. Today we face individualism in the industrialized countries of the world, often called "the North," and destroyed community in the poorest, least industrialized countries of the world, often called "the South." The Anabaptist vision once more will call us to break down artificial barriers by identifying with those who have been isolated by race, color, position, resources, or gender; by building community among those who have been isolated or whose community has been destroyed; and by challenging society to live by mutual love and respect.

There are such movements alive in the world today, and Anabaptists are in a peculiar position to act as agents for the changes that are already taking place.

Rather quietly, almost unnoticed by many Christians in the North, an ecclesiastical revolution has been taking place. Christians in the South are living out of new forms of the church, what we call base communities or *comunidades eclesiales de base* (CEBs). While not organically connected to the Anabaptist tradition, they reveal many remarkable similarities.

The term *base* refers to grassroots; like those of the Anabaptists, the new "churches" have emerged from among lay people as community organizations with a strong faith dimension.[31] Since 1968 CEBs have multiplied rapidly with a lay ministry, including catechetical instruction and evangelization.[32] CEBs are formed in much the same way that community organizations have been started in the North. Some agent raises consciousness among the people, who then determine their goals and organize for action. Of course, the agent (representing the Great Tradition) cannot determine the nature of these goals, since the base community, though usually attached to larger organizations, expresses local values (characteristics of the social matrix) rather than those of some outside power.

The community ministers to itself much as the believers minister to each other in the Anabaptist tradition.[33] Members of base communities care for one another and serve one another as ministers. Their Christology, like that of Anabaptists, depends not on the equation of a priest to Christ but on the equation of church community to the corporate body of Christ. Christ is present in the community rather than in the bishop or the sacrament.

The CEB understands itself as a church on the side of the poor, the weak, the disadvantaged, and the disenfranchised. Through CEBs people become actors in history rather than those who are acted upon.[34] Because present-day base communities often spring up among people who feel oppressed by the dominant system, theirs is a martyr community. Like the early Anabaptists, they are formed to be over against. Like Anabaptists, members of base communities suspect the institutions of the dominant society and, like the first Christians, they often are more aware of the demonic acting in social structures. This forces them to seek alternative plans.

Base communities not only stand over against but understand themselves as living in a type of exile or diaspora. Since they do not conform, they do not belong. CEBs are the first formal churches to emerge from the hegemony of Christendom.[35] In Christendom the dominant church participates in what some call the historic bloc.[36] Over the centuries the dominant church has learned to make peace with society by upholding its values and supporting a hierarchical system (though not necessarily a given hierarchy). The Christian tradition, as we have seen in the formation of the canon of the New Testament, eventually adjusts itself to the values and organization of the culture in which it participates. The base communities do not participate in this historic bloc and therefore, in a somewhat deconstructionist fashion, stand outside dominant society. As communities of mutual caring, Anabaptists have that same sense of not belonging to the hegemony.

In the story of Christendom there are numerous examples of movements that have broken with the tradition. The importance of Anabaptism and the base community is, in part, that there is no sharp break with the Great Tradition. Their so-called error is the break with the church's rapprochement with society. They seek another social form, not another tradition. In other words, they consider themselves to be actively engaged with the Christian tradition. Base communities are in active communication with the larger churches from which they came and welcome the presence of the church and its personnel, if the latter are willing to adapt to new forms of ministry and can refrain from making authoritative judgments on the basis of outside value systems.

CEBs are strongly attached to the Great Tradition and even more so to the Bible. Community interpretation of Bible stories raises social awareness and helps set new directions. The community acts with a sense of both the biblical tradition and their present situation.[37] Biblical stories, told in the community, melt quickly into the circumstances in which the community finds itself. Sometimes the biblical story is barely discernible. For interpretation of the Bible historical considerations and critical observations may become unimportant. Nevertheless, the power of the narrative remains in the community. Just as Jesus is present when the community assembles as the corporate body of Christ, just as Christ is present at the Eucharist when the community breaks the bread, so the Bible is inspired when the community receives it. At this crucial point Anabaptism and Christian base communities come together.

Base communities are not Anabaptist intentional communities. While mutual caring will go on, there is not intentional corporate ownership of resources. Nevertheless, base communities intend to include everyone without regard for wealth, education, or whatever class distinctions might exist in the dominant culture.

Given these traditional concerns it is not surprising that Anabaptists have already moved in the direction of community wellness programs like those established in CEBs. For an indication of what the future holds, we will look rather closely at some Anabaptist programs as they have emerged in the last few years.

·8·

Communities of Wellness

Both Mennonites and Brethren have actively worked at developing community health programs for areas of the world that lack appropriate health care. The Mennonites particularly have developed program manuals that provide the opportunity of reduplicating wellness programs throughout the Third World. Brethren developed a program in Nigeria that has become a model for some groups and recently has been adapted to First World communities.

The Brethren program entitled Lafiya suggests the future of health programs within the Anabaptist tradition and those with similar convictions. Brethren first developed mission work in the northeastern state of Nigeria known in Hausa as Lardin Gabas. The first two missionaries, Stover Kulp and Albert Helser, began a medical program in 1923. Though not specifically trained in medicine (Helser had taken a course of studies in tropical medicine), they reported that they were dispensing medicine and treating twenty to thirty patients a day even before they could speak Hausa.[1] The next year they were joined by a prominent service-oriented physician, Homer Burke. That initial program eventually resulted in the building of two general hospitals (one at Garkida and one at Lassa), a leprosy hospital at Virgwi, seven village dispensaries, and three maternity clinics. On the ecclesiastical level ninety-six congregations were formed with about forty thousand members. Brethren schools were founded (primarily Kulp Bible School), and the Church of the Brethren also participates in the Theological College of Northern Nigeria. By comity agreement the Brethren, called *Ekklesiyar 'Yan'uwa a Nigeria* in Hausa, are responsible for the area called Lardin Gabas.

The hospitals are constantly overloaded. At Garkida in 1970 (before Lafiya) there were more than one hundred patients but just eighty beds. During that year there were 530 deliveries, 938 minor surgical operations, and 416 major operations. Over 93,000 persons sought assistance at the hospital. There was one doctor. The Lassa hospital, with sixty beds, was a more modern facility than Garkida, but in 1970 it had no doctor. A Nigerian pastor who was also a registered nurse administered the medical work, with the aid of twenty-two staff members. The system for medical delivery was intolerable. In 1970 there were five doctors, all expatriates, for the total population of Lardin Gabas. That amounted to about one doctor per 200,000 people (compared to one per every 660 in the United States). The Brethren determined that there must be a better way. Besides inadequate physician and hospital resources, there were other reasons to develop a new program.

The existing system was inefficient. In one area the infant mortality rate was a staggering 282 per 1,000.[2] An expatriate pediatrician saw that there were three major killers, two of which, malaria and dysentery, could be fairly easily recognized. He enlisted some young women at the local mission school to serve as health workers and taught them basic skills. They learned to recognize malaria by feeling the spleen, and dysentery by looking at the stool, and they learned to dispense the appropriate medication for each. The system was rough and the possibility for error was great, but the infant mortality rate fell to 78 deaths per 1,000. Observers have noted frequently that in Africa 80 to 90 percent of illnesses could be treated by local auxiliary medical personnel. The hospital system, with its very sparse resources, simply cannot reach enough people.

The hospital system was also an expensive type of health care. A contemporary study in Kenya showed that illnesses treated in a local dispensary cost 23 cents while the same illness in a primary health center cost 56 cents. The expense of hospital care itself rose quite rapidly. A district hospital would charge $11.80 to treat the illness; a regional hospital charged $24 for treatment of the same illness; and the cost rose to $52 at a central hospital. Not only were hospitals more expensive than primary health centers, but they were inaccessible for many local people, whose health problems simply went untreated. It would be more practical to train local nurses than to maintain an expensive hospital system.

Hospital treatment was also an alien system. Isolation of the patient from the village (or tribal) community tends to create even more ill health. Even though some hospitals make housing provisions for families and depend on relatives for food preparation, still the system works against holistic health. Most of the doctors are expatriates. While they are incredibly good at serving local populations, they are not tribal medicine women or men. They lack the relational charisma so often necessary for healing.

Local treatment is more efficient, less expensive, and more in tune with village life. A local program would also allow greater attention to preventing disease, not just curing it. Health care workers knew there was little value in treating people for dysentery if they continued to drink from a pool of standing water.

For these reasons in 1972 Brethren decided to inaugurate a local health program in the Lardin Gabas region. They were determined to raise over $1,000,000 to upgrade the physical plants of the hospitals, intensify training programs at the Lassa hospital, and develop a rural wellness program. In Hausa the word of greeting is *Lafiya* ('la-fee-ya), which means, "Are you well?" One normally responds with the same word, meaning "I am well." But the greeting is more than a social convention. It refers to the condition of one's family and relatives and as such takes precedence over any other form of business. Brethren decided to call the new health program Lafiya.

The Rural Health Program, developed by physician John Horning, proceeded in this way: a village was approached by the administrators of the program to determine if villagers wanted it. Normally the program would be explained by means of a parable, riddle, story, joke, or song. A typical parable ran something like this:

> A village in this region had a serious difficulty. There were several bandits living outside the village. Every week some of them would come into the village to pilfer food and livestock. When villagers tried to defend their homes, they were often hurt. So the villagers built special huts to care for the people who were hurt. This went on for years. One day a stranger came to the village and was shown around. When he saw the special huts he asked what they were for. The villagers said they held people who had been hurt when the bandits came to rob them. The stranger was surprised and asked, "Instead of building huts to care for those hurt, why don't you go out and drive away the bandits or capture them?"

If the village was interested in the program, then the details were made clear and a local rural health committee was formed (Brethren seem to favor committees over congregations).

The committee would then appoint a man and a woman to serve as village health workers (VHW). These persons had to be healthy and mature. They needed to be good storytellers and persons who could in their communication relate well to the customs and belief systems of their village. They also were required to pass literacy examinations in Hausa. Once approved they would be given a three-month intensive training course at Garkida. The trainees' expenses ($76.80) had to be paid by the village; this contribution showed that the village did indeed wish to participate in the Rural Health Program. Trainees had to collect the money from the villagers and pay for the training in advance.[3] The local committee and the trainee made a contract covering conditions of employment and setting a salary of $19.20 a month. At the training center the two villagers were taught the art of storytelling, basics in health education, and disease prevention. They learned what to recommend when a villager got sick and to refer patients with illnesses beyond their training to one of the hospitals. At the end of the three-month course the trainees returned to their village, where a health center had been built and stocked with supplies and equipment.

The range of this health program can be seen from the following activities:

1. A monthly "well-baby" or "under-five" clinic where infants and toddlers are screened for malnutrition or malaria. Very soon after the Lafiya program started there were eight thousand children involved. In the Uba district more than half the twelve thousand "under-fives" received recommended inoculations through the Lafiya program.

2. Prenatal clinics attended by midwives trained through the Lafiya program. In addition to examinations and advice, minerals and vitamins are dispensed. One team soon had three hundred mothers seeking its services.

3. Acting of skits and telling of health and wellness stories at market-day teaching sessions.

4. Development of health clubs or groups for men and for women where wellness teaching can be disseminated. This often occurred in the evening when stories would normally have been told. In essence wellness motifs are inserted into the pool of oral tradition.

The Rural Health Program established a system of wellness self-help that continues to function in remote Nigerian villages. Lafiya attracted the attention of other agencies and was heavily subsidized by the German Evangelical Churches' Central Agency for Development (EZE) and the Basel Mission. In 1989 there were sixty-seven active village health posts in the Lardin Gabas area. The communities are involved, and health has, for the most part, improved dramatically.[4]

On the one hand, Lafiya carries out the Anabaptist tradition, and yet, on the other, it points in a new direction. Lafiya demonstrates well the nature of mutual caring. The story of the bandits illustrates the difference between compassionate service and mutuality. Some groups would help the villagers by sending money to buy replacements for what was stolen, some would send personnel and equipment to build better first-aid stations, but the mutual assistance calls for cooperative action to rid the area of robbers. That mutuality would leave the village capable of warding off any future bandits. In that sense the Rural Health Program is an extension of mutual caring into the larger community. Brethren took upon themselves a Christian witness in Lardin Gabas, Nigeria. Eventually, they also shared responsibility for the wellness of the people — whether Christian or Muslim. Discipleship has indeed become responsible. Discipleship builds community.

Such programs reflect a shift in the relationship between religion and health in Anabaptist thought. Today the Anabaptist message is less a call to suffering discipleship than a call to the good life. Wellness programs seek to assure a long life free of illness; they try to build positive attitudes that can either abolish stress or handle it, long-lasting support groups, and disciplined moments of faith. It hardly seems like the church of the martyrs where death was around the corner and suffering was an expected part of life. What has happened? Perhaps an analogy will explain it. During World War II some Anabaptist types penned a document for the World Council of Churches entitled "War Is Contrary to the Will of God." A somewhat sympathetic World Council asked, in return, for a positive statement from the Anabaptists (or peace churches). In the late 1950s, in conjunction with the European-American Puidoux conferences (theological seminars on peace), Anabaptists produced a second document entitled "Peace Is the Will of God." Is not the theological shift signaled in this response? It is no longer sufficient to stand over against society and say, "Domination is contrary to the will of God." Now we must say, "Abundant life (wellness) is the will of God." Once abundant life has become the goal of life (vis-à-vis discipleship) the nature of conflict does change. The great enemy still exists, but it is no longer the state as such. Now it is multinational corporations (which have replaced the state as the ultimate pejorative term) and large manufacturers that have produced unhealthy products and that pollute the world God has given to our care.

Lafiya was a success. When, in 1990, the Association of Brethren Caregivers determined that a congregational wellness program should be its primary task, it went back to Lafiya for models and inspiration. This new Lafiya now operates in the Church of the Brethren.

Congregational Health

Wellness Programs

Since the early 1980s Mennonite Mutual Aid (MMA), at the request of the Mennonite Board of Missions, has been energetically involved in congregational wellness programs. Under the leadership of Ann Raber, MMA has developed comprehensive materials for preventive medicine and health. These materials have been utilized by Mennonite (and other) congregations primarily in the United States and Canada. Erland Waltner, a past president of the Mennonite Biblical Seminary, states well the positive basis for wellness: "The Bible values health,...teaches an implicit positive theology of the human body and offers to us an invitation to live human life to the full."[5] Willard Krabill, a key advisor for the wellness program, says the goal is "the abundant life Christ envisioned for us in John 10:10.... 'The thief comes only to steal and kill and destroy. I came that they may have life, and have it abundantly.'"[6] At the same time Krabill articulates an Anabaptist perspective with his final goal statement: "We strive for wellness...not as an end in itself but as a means of achieving our purpose in life and of fulfilling God's purposes in our world."[7]

The program, entitled RENEW (for Recreation, Education, Nutrition, Exercise, Wellness), is offered to all congregations.[8] Those who want it send trainees to a workshop led by one of the MMA personnel. These trainees then take the program to the congregation for eight weekly sessions, one for each aspect of the wellness program. Each session also includes an hour of supervised exercising. The eight aspects of the program are an expansion of the five originally proposed by Donald Ardell, an eminent authority in health planning: self-responsibility, nutritional awareness, physical fitness, stress management, and environmental sensitivity.[9] These have been expanded to include a more holistic approach (spiritual, physical, and psychological) with an Anabaptist "tenor" (social, relational, and vocational). The eight dimensions, outlined in the program's *Congregational Wellness Manual*, are as follows:

Spiritual

Professing personal faith and belief in Christ.

Making choices from a faith commitment perspective.

Accepting personal responsibility for those choices.

Mental

> Growing in self-understanding.
>
> Expressing emotions clearly, especially love and affirmation.
>
> Learning to express anger constructively.
>
> Responding positively to life experiences.

Relational

> Building strong relationships within family, church and community.
>
> Sharing in one-to-one and group situations.

Vocational

> Finding satisfaction in a chosen vocation.
>
> Balancing work, service and leisure time.

Physical

> Respecting, accepting and enjoying the body.
>
> Providing sufficient exercise and healthful nutrition for daily fitness.

Psychological

> Possessing inner peace for times of change and crisis.
>
> Coping with daily pressures and expectations.

Environmental

> Accepting responsibility for wise use of the earth's resources.
>
> Developing personal strategy to reduce consumption.

Social

> Living with a sense of purpose and direction.
>
> Having clear personal values and priorities.[10]

Based as it is on a general wellness program, the Mennonite program has widespread usefulness. But it also has an Anabaptist flavor in many places. Of course, there is a strong emphasis on community and support groups. The program's emphasis on relationships reflects deeply the communitarian nature of the Anabaptist vision. Of primary importance is the relationship to God: "The Christian life begins with this faith relationship in God through Christ. We offer ourselves to Him in obedience, loyalty, prayer and praise. In turn, we receive grace which affects our other relationships. Our faith relationship grows through sharing and serving, living and loving, hurting and hoping. To give and receive love becomes the central expression of our relationship with God and others."[11] Faith in God leads to mutuality: "The ability to love and accept love is foundational for happiness. It produces positive emotional responses. With it we find freedom to discuss our feelings. We build self-esteem and discover confidence when giving of ourselves. We develop the strength to confront and support. We express concern for another's personal well-being. Through all this, God's presence is experienced." At the heart of wellness is the sense of belonging, and belonging means primarily the church relationship:

> Ultimate supportive relationships are experienced in the church. The church provides a rich context for inspiration and social action. Relationships developed and sustained by the church become outlets for expressing personal beliefs and values. Without relationships we cannot cope with life. *Our personal happiness has more to do with how frequently we are sick and how quickly we get well than do our genes and body chemistry, diet or environment* [emphasis added]. *Our positive relationships are as important as three regular meals a day* [emphasis in original].

The connection between religion and medicine in the Anabaptist tradition could not be better stated than this. Satisfactory relationships in the community of faith produce health.

The *Wellness Manual* deals extensively with Anabaptist tendencies like overwork and overeating, discussing them as stress factors. In the "Physical" section the manual deals quite explicitly with proper diet, even giving tables regarding fat, fiber, protein, and cholesterol. Yet it is interesting that the manual recognizes the importance of eating together as the way of building the very community that creates wellness:

> Wellness presupposes that nutrition is more than the sum of the parts of the food we eat. The eating and drinking of communion commemorates a wellness that grew out of Jesus' suffering and death.... This eating and

drinking in the context of the story of Jesus forms the central part of our worship. We partake in the wholeness given the church.

Within view of the divine plan for our lives, our eating takes on not just a mechanical function, but allows us to express our relationships within our families, extended circle of friends, church. We eat and drink daily with each other as unto the Lord. Some of us have learned to connect food and love in our minds; we prepare and serve food to family and friends to show our love.[12]

The congregational wellness program is explicit, aggressive, and persuasive, but not ideological. Health does not derive strictly from exercise, diet, prayer, or relaxation. Health derives from a satisfactory relationship with God, the body of Christ.

Congregational Health Care Committees

Lartia, a long-time member of First Church of the Brethren, was told by her physician she had cancer. Chemotherapy was prescribed. She was deeply troubled, even frightened. The pastor called together a small group of her friends along with some who had knowledge about health care. The group offered care and support and then prayed with her. As the treatments progressed, Lartia found she could not recuperate from one session to the next. She was constantly fatigued and nauseated. Furthermore, her fingers were so badly burned that they became raw. The support group met again and suggested she seek another opinion about the progression of the treatment. She did as her church group suggested. Another procedure was found, and she successfully completed the necessary treatments.

Lartia's story illustrates how, for the Anabaptist, the entire faith community should participate in wellness. But in our individualistic society that is not always possible. Anabaptists suggest that some persons might take the lead in congregational wellness strategies. In the local congregation the health care committee can support and advise members regarding health procedures and alternative possibilities. The committee can share the latest health information, such as appropriate foods or exercises. The committee can act as congregational advocates for a better environment and for better care by society of those who are deprived or disadvantaged. The committee would function almost like the earlier deacons and deaconesses.[13]

As has been seen so often in this study, Anabaptists believe that the individual is indivisible from the matrix that formed him or her. It seems illogical, even destructive, to separate a person from that community when health decisions need to be made. So Anabaptists recommend not only a congregational health care committee but also ethics committees for hospitals and other health care institutions. For a specific patient the ethics committee should be composed of the attending physician, a neutral physician, an institutional administrator, a nurse, a member of the family, and a member of the congregational health care committee. The ethics committee should have not only the right to discuss and influence prognoses and treatments but the right to act on behalf of the patient. If this were legally acceptable, and it should be, cases of heroic measures like the Quinlan case could be decided by a committee, including the patient's formative community, instead of waiting for permission from the patient that can never come. If persons cannot trust their lives with family and community, then an acceptable quality of life has already disappeared and death has taken over.

At the same time the ethics committee should be aware of the social implications of any procedure recommended for the patient. Can the patient and family afford the pain and cost of a potential treatment like a kidney transplant or a bone marrow transplant? Must rising insurance and medical costs be held in check at some point? There is no reason to leave a person alone to make these decisions. The individual's reasoning process and ethical standards were created by the community. Life-and-death decisions should occur in the same context, especially if the patient is not physically or emotionally capable of discerning the best communal procedure.[14]

National Health System

I wonder what would happen if Anabaptists could formulate and enforce national health policies. Anabaptists do occasionally speak to national policy. Both Mennonites and Brethren have made statements about the national health crisis. The Mennonites (through Mennonite Mutual Aid) have also produced a four-session study guide to enable Mennonites to understand how they, as Christians, fit into present health programs and what goals for health care they should seek in the political arena. Anabaptists would agree, more or less, on the following four points:

Justice. There should be universal health care regardless of ability to pay. The treatment of individuals should be placed in the larger context of caring for one another.

Acceptance of mortality. Death should be acknowledged as an inevitable part of life, so that attempts to save life should not be exaggerated. Resources spent on heroic measures and the "last year of life" should be spent on other social problems.

Health promotion. Individuals should be encouraged to take responsibility for a healthy lifestyle. At the same time there should be considerable emphasis on wellness education and community-based primary care.

Quality care with controlled cost. The system should promote quality of life, not quantity. Costs should be cut by simplifying administration, reducing the excessiveness of malpractice litigation, and avoiding unwarranted defensive medicine.[15]

The Individual

Even though he or she is formed by the Anabaptist community, the individual finally must make a choice for health and act upon that decision. Mennonites and Brethren urge members to make decisions in advance regarding the use of their organs and the extent of heroic measures. As a way of summarizing the relation of religion and health in the Anabaptist tradition, I offer a positive health and lifestyle pledge for each individual to consider:

1. I am one with the human race.

2. I commit my mind, body, and spirit to health and wholeness.

3. I will live cheerfully and simply by sharing my gifts and resources with those who need them.

4. I will work with others to influence the medical and religious communities to provide more equal opportunity and access to necessary resources so that we all may participate and grow more fully in our Christian lives.

5. I will not knowingly create products which cause harm to others.

6. I will manage my time responsibly, striving to achieve a balance of work, relaxation, creativity, and rest.

7. I will keep my body nutritionally well, and will practice physical fitness consistent with my personal needs.

8. I will strive for regular physical evaluations by medically trained professionals, for continuing religious experiences with concerned Christians, and for open and honest communication with my family and friends.

9. I will practice daily personal renewal through Bible study, meditation, and prayer.

10. I will participate fully in the peoplehood and servanthood of the family of God.[16]

Community Means Health

From its inception in the sixteenth century Anabaptism has been a communitarian form of the Christian tradition. That sense of community has encompassed fairly clear theological (New Testament–based), socio-logical, and economic dimensions. Theologically, Anabaptists intended to live their faith out of their understanding of the New Testament and the life of the early Christian church. Sociologically, this faith conviction en-gendered a form of community that broke ranks with both Catholic and Protestant understandings of church and society. Economically, by shar-ing goods and services the new communities offered a radical alternative to feudalism and eventually capitalism itself. Throughout the succeeding centuries these original elements have often become blurred, have inter-twined in different patterns, and have been adapted to many different social matrices. Sometimes Anabaptists withdrew into intentional commu-nities; sometimes they created subcultures within the dominant culture; sometimes they acted prophetically as counterculture groups; sometimes they lived physically apart from and yet still participated in their heritage; sometimes they were absorbed into the mainstream.

Living in a communitarian context meant subordinating self to the faith community, its immediate programs, and its end-time goals. Birth is entrance into the community; death separates one from community; resur-rection returns one to community. Decisions regarding birth, illness, and death are considered in light of the community. Alienation from the com-munity brings dishonor, isolation, and illness. Peace with the community brings honor, satisfaction, and health.

For the most part living in community was intimately tied to health. At first the Anabaptists, especially the Hutterites, were a unique medical community.[17] They believed in a caring God, the goodness of humanity, and the efficacy of human relationships. In such an atmosphere, unham-pered by supernaturalism and any inherent connection between sin and health, rational types of medical practice could flourish. Over the years, as the Anabaptists developed into somewhat ingrown communities and created subcultures, strong elements of folk medicine appeared (especially in those groups touched by the Pennsylvania Dutch subculture). In some Anabaptist groups, primarily the Mennonites, shamans became popular, and in all groups the use of natural medicines was practiced. Some groups, like the Brethren, turned to representative leaders of the community instead of shamans for healing. Although some leaders used folk medicine, most worked for reconciliation and the return of the ill person to healthy community relationships (seen primarily in the service of anointing).

About the end of the nineteenth century globalization began to affect Anabaptist attitudes and practices deeply. When, with other Western churches, Anabaptists also turned to a program of global missions, they invariably included in their mission teams doctors, health practitioners, and agricultural experts.[18] Hospitals were built around the world and populated in part by Western personnel. Even more significant changes occurred in the twentieth century. As a result of the two world wars Anabaptists came to see firsthand the pain and suffering of the world at large. They responded with massive projects like the Heifer Project and the Christian Rural Overseas Project, designed to alleviate the suffering of humanity and to bring health to all peoples. The community of faith had extended itself to a global community.

Anabaptism stands now at a crossroads. Either it can live in enclaves, which may lead to the group's extinction, or it can give to the world what it first gave in the sixteenth century: new communities of faith that are at the same time communities of health and caring. The new vision depends on a fresh look at the Jesus of the New Testament. There we find a tradition about Jesus that did, indeed, show the primary roles of disciples to be healing the sick and forming a community. By breaking down artificial barriers between clean and unclean and by creating bonds across class distinctions, the disciples of Jesus created new communities that were close-knit yet universal to the core.

In our day similar communities are being formed throughout the world, the most prominent of which are called base communities. Anabaptists of the twenty-first century will surely join hands with this upsurge in primary health communities.[19] Already Anabaptists have developed preventive health groups in various parts of the world. In North America they have developed serious, effective congregational wellness programs. The future direction of Anabaptism has not been determined, nor even clearly formulated. But given the Anabaptist heritage it seems inevitable that such communities will be created. Improvement in world health will emerge from these developing communities of faith.

Notes

Chapter 1 / The Anabaptist Vision

1. Walter Klaassen, *Anabaptism: Neither Catholic nor Protestant*, rev. ed. (Waterloo, Canada: Conrad Press, 1981), p. 1.

2. Eusebius, *Ecclesiastical History* 4:22, 4.

3. Biblical citations are from the New Revised Standard Version unless otherwise indicated.

4. Ernst Käsemann, "Ketzer und Zeuge. Zum johannischen Verfasserproblem," *Zeitschrift für Theologie und Kirche* 48 (1951): 292–311. For further reflection see Rudolf Bultmann, *The Johannine Epistles* (Philadelphia: Fortress, 1973), pp. 100–101.

5. Elaine Pagels, *The Gnostic Gospels* (New York: Random House, 1979), pp. 28–47. See also Karen Jo Torjeson, *When Women Were Priests: Women's Leadership in the Early Church and the Scandal of Their Subordination in the Rise of Christianity* (New York: HarperCollins, 1993), pp. 9–87.

6. Peter Brown, *The Cult of the Saints* (Chicago: University of Chicago Press, 1981).

7. Graydon F. Snyder, *Ante Pacem: Archaeological Evidence of Church Life before Constantine* (Macon, Ga.: Mercer University Press, 1985), pp. 87–92.

8. Gottfried Arnold, *Unpartheyische Kirchen=und Ketzer=Historie, Vom Anfang des Neuen Testaments bis auf das Jahr Christi 1688* (Frankfurt am Main: Thomas Fritschens sel. Erben, 1729). In a harsh way Arnold (p. 154) reflects the early Anabaptist view: "die welt sey nun des satans eigen, und die kirche sey gleichsam zu einem hurenhause worden" (the world now belongs to satan, and the church has become a whorehouse).

9. Murray L. Wagner, *Peter Chelcicky: A Radical Separatist in Hussite Bohemia* (Scottdale, Pa.: Herald Press, 1983).

10. Walter Klaassen, "Anabaptism," *Mennonite Encyclopedia* 5:23–26.

11. George H. Williams, *The Radical Reformation* (Philadelphia: Westminster Press, 1962), pp. 120–27.

12. From the Hutterian *Chronicle* as quoted in Donald F. Durnbaugh, *The Believers' Church: The History and Character of Radical Protestantism* (New York: Macmillan, 1968), p. 85.

13. Direct connections with the Peasants' War are difficult to prove, yet it is clear that some early preachers like Balthasar Hubmaier were involved. More apocalyptic types like Hans Hut thought the conflict marked the advent of the end time. See James M. Stayer, "Peasants' War," *Mennonite Encyclopedia* 5:687–88.

14. Max Weber, *General Economic History* (New York: Collier, 1961), p. 68.

15. Karl Mannheim, *Ideology and Utopia* (New York: Harcourt Brace, 1936), p. 212.

16. Dale Brown, *Understanding Pietism* (Grand Rapids, Mich.: Eerdmans, 1977).

17. See Franklin H. Littell, *The Anabaptist View of the Church*, vol. 8 of Studies in Church History, ed. James H. Nichols and Wilhelm Pauck (American Society of Church History, 1952), p. xi.

18. The Anabaptist groups respect each other and often are in close fellowship. As will be seen, Mennonites and Brethren have often cooperated in programs, for example, in worldwide service projects. Sometimes the distinctive character of each branch may not be fully recognized. In a remarkable speech before the ninth conference on Mennonite Educational and Cultural Problems (Hesston College, Hesston, Kansas, 1953), Harold Bender, who defined the Anabaptist vision for this generation, described some outside influences that are destructive for the Mennonites. He called for, among other things, "a clearly thought out and consistent theological line, not a mixture of confused theologies borrowed from other groups and movements. Let us work together for this. Let us take the lesson from other groups, such as the Church of the Brethren, who are in considerable dilemma in several respects because of their failure to do this very thing in their theology." See p. 40 of the *Proceedings of the Ninth Conference on Mennonite Educational and Cultural Problems* (North Newton, Ks.: Mennonite Press, 1953).

19. Karl A. Peter, *The Dynamics of Hutterite Society* (Edmonton, Alberta: University of Alberta Press, 1987), p. 8.

20. Lewis A. Coser, *Greedy Institutions: Patterns of Undivided Commitment* (New York: Free Press, 1974), p. 105.

21. *The Bloody Theater or Martyrs' Mirror of the Defenseless Christians* [1660], ed. Thieleman J. van Braght (Scottdale, Pa.: Herald Press, 1972), p. 741 (hereafter cited as *Martyrs' Mirror*).

22. Littell, *Anabaptist View*, p. 50.

23. Harold Bender, "The Anabaptist Vision," *Church History* 13 (1944): 3–24.

24. See the historical study by William Klassen, *Covenant and Community: The Life and Writings of Pilgram Marpeck* (Grand Rapids, Mich.: Eerdmans, 1968), pp. 77–87. Perry Yoder speaks of Anabaptist congregations as "hermeneutical communities"; see Yoder, "The Role of the Bible in Mennonite Self-Understanding," in *Mennonite Identity: Historical and Contemporary Perspectives*, ed. Calvin W. Redekop and Samuel J. Steiner (Lanham, Md.: University Press of America, 1988), p. 76.

25. The term *Mennonite* has been used as a verb meaning to travel from place to place inexpensively by staying with other members of the faith community, hence the phrase "to mennonite around the country."

26. It is important to note that Anabaptists were not alone in their anti-intellectualism and concern for restitutionism. Erasmus wrote to John Colet, the new, radical dean of St. Paul's Cathedral: "Theology is the mother of sciences. But nowadays the good and the wise keep clear of it, and leave the field to the dull and sordid, who think themselves omniscient. You have taken arms against these people [theologians and intellectuals]. You are trying to bring back the Christianity of the apostles, and clear away the thorns and briars with which it is overgrown"; James A. Froude, *Life and Letters of Erasmus* (New York: Scribner's Sons, 1894), p. 48.

Chapter 2 / Wholeness in Community

1. Walter Klaassen, "The Anabaptist Tradition," in *Caring and Curing: Health and Medicine in the Western Religious Traditions*, ed. Ronald L. Numbers and Darrel W. Amundsen (New York: Macmillan, 1986), p. 275.

2. Bruce J. Malina, *The New Testament World: Insights from Cultural Anthropology* (Atlanta: John Knox Press, 1981).

3. Mary Douglas, *Natural Symbols: Explorations in Cosmology* (New York: Pantheon Books, Random House, 1970). For an excellent review see Sheldon R. Isenberg and Dennis E. Owen, "Bodies, Natural and Contrived: The Work of Mary Douglas," *Religious Studies Review* 3 (1977): 1–17.

4. One might add that sickness is the process whereby behavioral and biological signs are given socially recognizable meanings. The total composite of disease, illness, and sickness describes an unhealthy person. These definitions are taken from medical anthropology; see, for example, George M. Foster and Barbara Gallatin Anderson, *Medical Anthropology* (New York: John Wiley and Sons, 1978), p. 146; George Murdock, *Theories of Illness: A World Survey* (Pittsburgh: University of Pittsburgh Press, 1980); and John Dominic Crossan, *The Historical Jesus: The Life of a Mediterranean Jewish Peasant* (San Francisco: Harper, 1991), pp. 336–37.

5. The Greek term for reconciliation, *katallage*, suggests mutuality in self-limitation, while the Latin term *reconcilium* has more the sense of arbitration.

6. Crossan, *Historical Jesus*, pp. 316–18; Paul W. Hollenbach, "Jesus, Demoniacs, and Public Authorities: A Socio-Historical Study," *Journal of the American Academy of Religion* 99 (1981): 567–88.

7. The powwower almost always deals with illness rather than disease, natural problems rather than accidents. See John A. Hostetler, "Folk and Scientific Medicine in Amish Society," *Human Organization* 22 (1963–64): 269–75.

8. The term *powwow* was first used by New England Puritans to refer to healing. Apparently it was used by Algonquin Native Americans to refer to gesticulations of their medicine men. Pennsylvania Germans also used the German term *braucher* (one who uses sympathy healing). See Gerald C. Studer, "Powwowing: Folk Medicine or White Magic?" *Pennsylvania Mennonite Heritage* 3 (July 1980): 17–23.

9. Barbara Louise Reimensnyder, *Powwowing in Union County: A Study of Pennsylvania German Folk Medicine in Context* (New York: AMS Press, 1989), pp. 44–45.

10. Patricia P. McKegney, *"Charm for Me, Mr. Eby..."* (Bamberg, Ontario: Bamberg Press, 1989). Her material comes from a collection of 224 letters dated from 1890 to 1920.

11. On remedies see McKegney, *"Charm for Me"*; Studer, "Powwowing"; Hostetler, "Folk and Scientific Medicine in Amish Society"; Klaassen, "Anabaptist Tradition," pp. 271–86.

12. McKegney, *"Charm for Me,"* p. 20.

13. McKegney, *"Charm for Me,"* p. 16.

14. The book *The Long Lost Friend* (Lancaster, Pa.: Johann Georg Hohman, 1865) was probably first published in English in 1856 and then again in 1863. Later books of Moses have long been associated with magical and healing arts. See Studer, "Powwowing"; John R. Colombo, "Moses in Waterloo County," *Waterloo Review* 2 (1960): 46; Carleton F. Brown, "The Long Hidden Friend," *Journal of American Folk-Lore* 17 (1904): 89; Thomas R. Brendle and Claude W. Unger, *Folk Medicine of the Pennsylvania Germans: The Non-Occult Cures* (New York: August M. Kelley, 1970), pp. 17–18.

15. Colombo, "Moses," p. 44.

16. W. J. Wintember, "German-Canadian Folk-Lore," Ontario Historical Society, *Papers and Records* 3 (1901): 87, quoted in McKegney, *"Charm for Me,"* p. 21.

17. *Inglenook Doctor Book* (Elgin, Ill.: Brethren Publishing House, 1903), p. 75.

18. Quoted in Reimensnyder, *Powwowing in Union County*, p. 12.

19. Alfred L. Shoemaker, *Traditional Rhymes and Jingles of the Pennsylvania Dutch* (Lancaster, Pa.: Pennsylvania Dutch Folklore Center, 1951), p. 9.

20. George Brunk II suspects that Mennonites, to their own detriment, failed to utilize fully the New Testament anointing service. That lack of a community healing service left open the need for shamans and charismatic faith healers. See Brunk, "Faith Healing," *Mennonite Encyclopedia* 5:288.

21. Graydon F. Snyder and Kenneth M. Shaffer, Jr., *Texts in Transit II* (Elgin, Ill.: Brethren Press, 1991), pp. 227–35.

22. Harold Z. Bomberger, *Brethren Encyclopedia*, s.v. "Anointing."

23. Warren F. Groff, *Story Time: God's Story and Ours* (Elgin, Ill.: Brethren Press, 1974).

24. For the power of shame in affective or relational control see Donald Nathanson, *Shame and Pride: Affect, Sex, and the Birth of Self* (New York: W. W. Norton, 1992), pp. 19, 47–72. Shame occurs when something private becomes known by the community. In contrast, guilt occurs when a code has been violated. On shame in the Near East in contrast to the West see Jane Schneider, "Of Vigilance and Virgins: Honor, Shame and Access to Resources in Mediterranean Societies," *Ethnology* 9 (1971): 1–24, especially pp. 17–23.

25. Graydon F. Snyder, *Brethren Encyclopedia*, s.v. "Covenant Theology"; Snyder and Shaffer, *Texts in Transit II*, pp. 209–16.

26. Inez Long, "Can Brethren Repent?" *Gospel Messenger* 106, no. 39 (12 October 1957), pp. 3, 4, 8, 9. She concludes that Brethren, and of course Anabaptists in general, do not have an ethos that leads to repentance.

Chapter 3 / The Family of God

1. See John W. Miller, *A Christian Approach to Sexuality* (Scottdale, Pa.: Mennonite Publishing House, 1973), pp. 35–38; Roland H. Bainton, *Women of the Reformation* (Minneapolis: Augsburg Publishing, 1971), pp. 9–14.

2. Snyder, *Brethren Encyclopedia*, s.v. "Covenant Theology."

3. Calvin Redekop, *Mennonite Society* (Baltimore: Johns Hopkins University Press, 1989), pp. 169–71.

4. Williams, *The Radical Reformation*, pp. 362–81.

5. Monika Elizabeth Trümpi, "With Our Tiniest," *Children in Community* (Rifton, N.Y.: Plough Publishing House, 1939), p. 18. See Bob Wagoner and Shirley Wagoner, *Community in Paraguay: A Visit to the Bruderhof* (Farmington, Pa.: Plough Publishing House, 1991), pp. 198–219. It should be noted that an intentional community called the Bruderhof, which originated in Germany in 1920, joined the Hutterites in 1974. These communities, called the eastern colonies, do not reflect the traditionalism of their Canadian counterparts, called the western colonies. The above material comes from the eastern group.

In 1995 it became clear that the Bruderhof differed with the Hutterites so significantly that unity was no longer possible. The major point of conflict originated in the concept of theocracy: human leadership or divine guidance? See "An Open Letter from the Bruderhof" written on behalf of all its members by J. Christoph Arnold, *Plough* 41 (Winter 1995): 2–6.

6. Karl Peter, "The Dialectic of Family and Community in the Social History of the Hutterites," in *The Canadian Family in Comparative Perspective*, ed. Lyle E. Larson (Scarborough, Ontario: Prentice-Hall of Canada, 1976), pp. 337–51.

7. *Martyrs' Mirror*, pp. 877–81, 882, 926.

8. Graydon F. Snyder, *Brethren Encyclopedia*, s.v. "Sexuality, Human." John Klassen, "Women and the Family among Dutch Anabaptist Martyrs," *Mennonite Quarterly Review* 60 (1986): 548–71.

9. The practice of ascetic sexuality did occur occasionally in Anabaptism. Note particularly the abortive experiment at Ephrata under Conrad Beissel; see Julie E. Riley, *Brethren Encyclopedia*, s.v. "Ephrata Community."

10. Dale Stoffer, *Background and Development of Brethren Doctrines, 1650–1987* (Philadelphia: Brethren Encyclopedia, 1989), p. 51.

11. Abbie C. Morrow, "Col. 3:18," *Gospel Herald* 8 (1915): 475–76.

12. Sharon Klingelsmith, "Women in the Mennonite Church, 1900–1930," *Mennonite Quarterly Review* 54 (1980): 163–207.

13. One Mennonite scholar, John W. Miller, has written a learned plea for the enhanced role of the father in the family; see Miller, "The Contemporary Fathering Crisis: The Bible and Research Psychology," *Conrad Grebel Review* 1 (1984): 21–37.

14. Melvin Gingerich, "Change and Uniformity in Mennonite Attire," *Mennonite Quarterly Review* 40 (1966): 243–59.

15. Donald B. Kraybill, "Mennonite Woman's Veiling: The Rise and Fall of a Sacred Symbol," *Mennonite Quarterly Review* 61 (1987): 298–320.

16. Leo Driediger and J. Howard Kauffman, in "Urbanization of Mennonites:

Canadian and American Comparisons," *Mennonite Quarterly Review* 52 (1982): 294–311, show that urban Mennonites have accepted divorce more readily than have their rural counterparts: 39 percent of the rural sampling saw no possibility of a divorce as compared to 24 percent of the urban. Nevertheless, the Mennonite family is quite stable. In a 1985 study 75.3 percent of all adult men (over twenty years of age) were married to their original spouse, and 67.1 percent of adult women were married to their original spouse. In the same study the percentage of divorced adults ran less than 2 percent. See Redekop, *Mennonite Society*, p. 170.

17. The complexity can be seen in a special issue of *Brethren Life and Thought* (no. 1, 1991). All of a variety of Brethren express concern and empathy for homosexuals. Some can countenance homosexual bonding, but others see no possibility.

18. J. Howard Kauffman and Leland Harder, *Anabaptists Four Centuries Later: A Profile of Five Mennonite and Brethren in Christ Denominations* (Scottdale: Herald Press, 1975). The authors found that 11 percent of Mennonites oppose the use of birth control devices by married spouses and 25 percent feel they are sometimes wrong; 17 percent were not certain. Thus, over half of those polled had at least a lingering doubt about the use of birth control devices (p. 180).

19. Kauffman and Harder show that most Mennonites reject a nontherapeutic abortion, but they are much more sympathetic to the mother whose health is at stake. The communitarian ethic is not absolute, but it does predictably protect the community (strongly pro-life unless the mother's well-being is at stake, and then more pro-choice; p. 181).

20. Menno Simons and other Anabaptists believed that Christ came to take away the sins of the whole world. The slate was wiped clean. To baptize infants violates the blood of Christ. See Williams, *The Radical Reformation*, p. 389.

21. Peter Rideman, *Account of Our Religion, Doctrine and Faith, Given by Peter Rideman of the Brothers Whom Men Call Hutterians* (London: Hodder and Stoughton, and Rifton, N.Y.: Plough Publishing House, 1950), p. 130. Rideman refers here to 1 Peter 3:18, where Christ is put to death in the flesh but made alive in the Spirit.

22. Eberhard Arnold, *Children's Education in Community: The Basis of Bruderhof Education* (Rifton, N.Y.: Plough Publishing House, 1976), p. 16.

23. Redekop, *Mennonite Society*, pp. 76–89.

24. See Joseph W. Eaton and Robert J. Weil, *Culture and Mental Disorders: A Comparative Study of the Hutterites and Other Populations* (Glencoe, Ill.: Free Press, 1955); see also Joseph W. Eaton, "Adolescence in a Communal Society," *Mental Hygiene* 48 (1964): 66–73.

25. John A. Hostetler, *Hutterite Society* (Baltimore: Johns Hopkins University Press, 1974), pp. 333–35.

26. Eaton, "Adolescence," p. 70.

27. Peter Rideman, *Account of Our Religion*, pp. 97–98.

28. Paul D. Simmons, *Birth and Death: Bioethical Decision-Making* (Philadelphia: Westminster, 1983), pp. 80–82. For a guarded Mennonite approbation of the

distinction, see John R. Burkholder, "A Theological Approach," in *Bioethics and the Beginning of Life: An Anabaptist Perspective*, ed. Roman J. Miller and Beryl H. Brubaker (Scottdale, Pa.: Herald Press, 1990), pp. 31–44.

29. Anne Krabill Hershberger, "Maternal Perspectives," in Miller and Brubaker, *Bioethics and the Beginning of Life*, pp. 144–53.

30. For a useful analysis of the options see Stanley J. Grenz, "Abortion: A Christian Response," *Conrad Grebel Review* 2 (1984): 21–30.

31. Minutes of the Annual Conference of the Church of the Brethren (1972). Donald E. Miller, *Brethren Encyclopedia*, s.v. "Abortion." Miller's statement that opposition to abortion depends on the sacredness of human life represents the impact of individualism on the Anabaptist tradition.

32. Hostetler, *Hutterite Society*, p. 203; John A. Hostetler, *Amish Society* (Baltimore: Johns Hopkins University Press, 1980), p. 101. John W. Bennett, *Hutterian Brethren: The Agricultural Economy and Social Organization of a Communal People* (Stanford: Stanford University Press, 1967), pp. 127, 164. Emmert F. Bittinger, *Brethren Encyclopedia*, s.v. "Birth Rate."

33. Enos D. Martin and Ruth K. Martin, "Psychological Perspectives," in Miller and Brubaker, *Bioethics and the Beginning of Life*, pp. 154–82.

34. About 80 percent of Amish children, for example, become Amish on a voluntary basis; see Hostetler, *Amish Society*, p. 106.

35. Hostetler, *Amish Society*, p. 102; Hostetler, *Hutterite Society*, p. 291.

36. Elisabeth Kübler-Ross, *Death: The Final Stage of Growth* (Englewood Cliffs, N.J.: Prentice-Hall, 1975).

37. At a Mennonite conference on health care in Indianapolis, 6 March 1992, two presenters addressed the issue of dying. Donald Steelberg said the medical systems in America cannot be reformed until we change our attitude toward death ("The Church Confronts Its Mission in Health and Healing," p. 6). Beryl Brubaker, in response, reflected on his experience with intensive care units and agreed that the scientific reductionism of medicine has made living a technological success requirement; he, too, called for a faith understanding of dying. The case is well stated by David Schroeder in "Life and Death: Biblical-Theological Perspectives," in *Medical Ethics, Human Choices: A Christian Perspective*, ed. John Rogers (Scottdale: Herald Press, 1988), pp. 63–72.

38. Dennis D. Martin, *Brethren Encyclopedia*, s.v. "Tobacco." For chemical dependency in more detail see Graydon F. Snyder, *Tough Choices: Health Care Decisions and the Faith Community* (Elgin, Ill.: Brethren Press, 1988), pp. 88–94.

39. Eaton and Weil, *Culture and Mental Disorders*, pp. 17–25.

40. Not every decision needs to be made anew every time. Anabaptist writers would likely agree with John Rawls that all ethical decisions need to be made each time, but that most ethical judgments can be repeated without a fresh process (rule ethic); see John Rawls, *A Theory of Justice* (Cambridge: Harvard University Press, 1971), p. 4.

41. Snyder, *Tough Choices*, pp. 109–15; Paul Hoffmann, "Genetic Engineering," in Rogers, *Medical Ethics*, pp. 113–19.

Chapter 4 / One and the Many

1. See Krister Stendahl, "The Apostle Paul and the Introspective Conscience of the West," in his book *Paul among Jews and Gentiles and Other Essays* (Philadelphia: Fortress Press, 1976), pp. 78–96.

2. Vernard Eller, *Christian Anarchy: Jesus' Primacy over the Powers* (Grand Rapids: Eerdmans, 1987).

3. Dale W. Brown, *Brethren Encyclopedia*, s.v. "Humility." J. Liechty, "Humility: The Foundation of Mennonite Religious Outlook in the 1860s," *Mennonite Quarterly Review* 54 (1980): 5–31.

4. Calvin Redekop, "The Mennonite Transformation: From Gelassenheit to Capitalism," in *Visions and Realities*, ed. Harry Loewen and Al Reimer (Winnipeg: Hyperion Press, 1985), p. 98.

5. Several Anabaptist groups practice the washing of feet at communion. This particular hymn comes from the tradition of the Church of the Brethren.

6. Communion hymn from eighteenth-century Brethren life (emphasis added); in Donald F. Durnbaugh, *European Origins of the Brethren* (Elgin, Ill.: Brethren Press, 1958), pp. 415–17.

7. See Snyder and Shaffer, *Texts in Transit II*, pp. 33–42. Emmert F. Bittinger, "The Simple Life: A Chapter in the Evolution of a Doctrine," *Brethren Life and Thought* 23 (1978): 104–14.

8. Ferdinand Tönnies, *Community and Society* (New York: Harper and Row, 1957).

9. Redekop takes these terms from the work by Frederick Tolles titled *Meeting House and Counting House: The Quaker Merchants of Colonial Philadelphia, 1682-1763* (Chapel Hill: University of North Carolina Press, 1948). See Redekop, "The Mennonite Transformation," in Loewen and Reimer, *Visions and Realities*, pp. 103–7.

10. Rideman, *Account of Our Religion*, p. 90.

11. H. C. Early, "What the Church Stands For: Her Doctrines," in *Two Centuries of the Church of the Brethren*, ed. D. L. Miller, 2d ed. (Elgin, Ill.: Brethren Publishing House, 1909), p. 148.

12. The *hos me* (as if not) passage of 1 Corinthians 7:32–35 calls for a "teleological suspension" of social values. See Graydon F. Snyder, *First Corinthians: A Faith Community Commentary* (Macon, Ga.: Mercer, 1992), pp. 110–16.

13. See especially Art Gish, *Beyond the Rat Race* (Scottdale, Pa.: Herald Press, 1973), but also Vernard Eller, *The Simple Life* (Grand Rapids, Mich.: Eerdmans, 1973), and Edward Ziegler, *Simple Living* (Elgin, Ill.: Brethren Press, 1974).

14. John W. Miller, "Christian Ethics and Current Economic Problems," in *The Church as a Witness in Society* (Winnipeg: Board of Christian Service, 1959), F-5 and F-8.

15. So defined by Roy Vogt, "Economic Questions and Mennonite Conscience," in *Call to Faithfulness*, ed. Henry Poettcker and Rudy Regehr (Winnepeg: Canadian Mennonite Bible College, 1972), pp. 157–66.

16. Adapted from Guy F. Hershberger, *The Way of the Cross in Human Relations* (Scottdale, Pa.: Herald Press, 1958), p. 220. See also Redekop, *Mennonite Society*, pp. 195–97.

17. Kauffman and Harder, *Anabaptists Four Centuries Later*, p. 287.

18. Carl Bowman, *Profile of the Church of the Brethren* (Elgin, Ill.: Brethren Press, n.d.), p. 20.

19. Elmer M. Ediger, "Roots of the Mennonite Mental Health Story," in *If We Can Love: The Mennonite Mental Health Story*, ed. Vernon H. Neufeld (Newton, Ks.: Faith and Life Press, 1983), pp. 3–28.

20. See Michel Foucault, *Madness and Civilization: A History of Insanity in the Age of Reason* (New York: Random House, 1973). pp. ix–xii.

21. Gregory Zilborg and George W. Henry, *A History of Medical Psychology* (New York: W. W. Norton, 1941), p. 572.

22. Ediger, "Roots," p. 10.

23. Bertram D. Smucker, "Visitation Report on Bethesda Hospital, Vineland, Ontario, March 28, 1946," unpublished.

24. Neufeld, *If We Can Love*, p. 323n.

25. Eaton and Weil, *Culture and Mental Disorders*, pp. 43–45. Joseph W. Eaton, "Folk Psychiatry," *New Society* 48 (29 August 1963): pp. 9–11. Joseph W. Eaton, Robert J. Weil, and Bert Kaplan, "The Hutterite Mental Health Study," *Mennonite Quarterly Review* 25 (1951): 47–65.

26. Eaton, Weil, and Kaplan, "The Hutterite Mental Health Study," p. 50.

27. Calvin Redekop, "Psychology Is the Worst Thing That Has Happened to the Mennonites," *Festival Quarterly* 9 (1982): 10. Al Dueck makes a similar point in his article "North American Psychology: Gospel of Modernity?" *Conrad Grebel Review* 3 (1985): 165–78.

28. Al Dueck, "Psychology and Mennonite Self-Understanding," in Redekop and Steiner, *Mennonite Identity*, pp. 203–24. About 6 percent of Mennonite college graduates are psychology majors.

Chapter 5 / To Heal the Broken

1. In contrast to medieval practices the system of Galen used observation techniques more like those of a modern scientist.

2. *The Chronicle of the Hutterian Brethren*, vol. 1 (Rifton, N.Y.: Plough Publishing House, 1987), pp. 487–88.

3. John L. Sommer, "Hutterite Medicine and Physicians in Moravia in the Sixteenth Century and After," *Mennonite Quarterly Review* 27 (1953): 111–27, and see also complementary remarks by Robert Friedmann, "Hutterite Physicians and Barber-Surgeons," *Mennonite Quarterly Review* 27 (1953): 128–36.

4. Williams, *Radical Reformation*, pp. 195–98.

5. John Horsch, *The Hutterian Brethren: 1528–1931* (1927; reprint New York: Garland Press, 1971), p. 38.

6. Sommer, "Hutterite Medicine," pp. 112–15. Adapted by Sommer from

Harold S. Bender, trans., "A Hutterite School Discipline of 1578 and Peter Scherer's Address of 1568 to the Schoolmasters," *Mennonite Quarterly Review* 5 (1931): 232–41.

7. Sommer, "Hutterite Medicine," pp. 114–15.

8. Quoted in Sommer, "Hutterite Medicine," p. 115.

9. H. Clair Amstutz, "Medicine," *Mennonite Encyclopedia* 3:550–51.

10. Taken from the archives of the Women's Missionary and Service Commission of the Mennonite Church. See Elaine Sommers Rich, *Mennonite Women: A Story of God's Faithfulness, 1683–1983* (Scottdale, Pa.: Herald Press, 1983), p. 169.

11. See the articles on the Fahrney family, *Brethren Encyclopedia*, s.v. "Fahrney."

12. Mary Sue H. Rosenberger, *Light of the Spirit: The Brethren in Puerto Rico, 1942–1992* (Elgin, Ill.: Association of Brethren Caregivers, 1992).

13. Menno Simons, "To the Common People," *The Complete Writings of Menno Simons* (Scottdale, Pa.: Herald Press, 1978), p. 214.

14. Quoted in Bernie Wiebe, "Health Services," *Mennonite Encyclopedia* 5:366.

15. Michael Frantz, *Einfältige Lehr-Betrachtung* (1770), trans. in *Colonial America*, ed. Donald F. Durnbaugh (Elgin, Ill.: Brethren Press, 1967), p. 453.

16. See the excellent series of statements from Anabaptists assembled by Donald F. Durnbaugh, *Every Need Supplied: Mutual Aid and Christian Community in the Free Church, 1525–1675* (Philadelphia: Temple University Press, 1974).

17. Amstutz, "Medicine," p. 551.

18. L. W. Shultz, "The Formation of the Brethren Service Committee," in *To Serve the Present Age*, ed. Donald F. Durnbaugh (Elgin, Ill.: Brethren Press, 1975), pp. 111–15, and Roger E. Sappington, *Brethren Social Policy, 1908–1958* (Elgin, Ill.: Brethren Press, 1961).

19. Paul Erb, *Orie O. Miller: The Story of a Man and an Era* (Scottdale, Pa.: Herald Press, 1969), p. 131. On the history of the Mennonite Central Committee see *The Mennonite Central Committee Story*, ed. Cornelius J. Dyck (Scottdale, Pa.: Herald Press, 1980–81), and Robert S. Kreider and Rachel Waltner Goossen, *Hungry, Thirsty, a Stranger: The MCC Experience* (Scottdale, Pa.: Herald Press, 1988).

20. Graydon F. Snyder, *Brethren Encyclopedia*, s.v. "Love Feast."

21. Grant M. Stoltzfus, "The Inception of NSBRO and CPS during World War II," in Durnbaugh, *To Serve the Present Age*, pp. 116–22. See also an informative volume by Albert N. Keim titled *The CPS Story: An Illustrated History of Civilian Public Service* (Intercourse, Pa.: Good Books, 1990). These two authors also cooperated in writing a history of the peace churches and American military conscription in this century; see Albert N. Keim and Grant M. Stoltzfus, *The Politics of Conscience: The Historic Peace Churches and America at War, 1917–1955* (Scottdale, Pa.: Herald Press, 1988).

22. See Donald F. Durnbaugh, *Pragmatic Prophet: The Life of Michael Robert Zigler* (Elgin, Ill.: Brethren Press, 1989), p. 323.

23. Cornelius J. Dyck, "Mennonite Central Committee," *Mennonite Encyclopedia* 5:562.

24. Snyder, "Covenant Theology."

25. Bender, "The Anabaptist Vision."

26. Alexander Mack, "Rights and Ordinances," in Donald F. Durnbaugh, *European Origins of the Brethren* (Elgin, Ill.: Brethren Press, 1958), p. 364.

27. One of the strongest directors of Brethren Service, W. Harold Row, spoke of the Brethren sense of *Nachfolge* as the biblical/theological impetus for service in this century. His remarks are found in "The Brethren and Biblical Ethics," in *Adventurous Future*, ed. Paul H. Bowman (Elgin, Ill.: Brethren Press, 1959), pp. 135–36.

28. While the rank and file of Anabaptists may not be in touch with process theology, the Whiteheadian sense of love as mutuality over against Lutheran agape may indeed have influenced Anabaptist thinkers in the last forty years.

29. For a classic discussion of Anabaptist ethics see John Howard Yoder, *The Christian Witness to the State* (Newton, Ks.: Faith and Life Press, 1964). The clear typological distinctions made by Yoder would not characterize many present-day Anabaptist thinkers.

30. John D. Metzler, Sr., "The CROP Idea," in Durnbaugh, *To Serve the Present Age*, pp. 148–54.

31. See Thurl Metzger, "The Heifer Project," in Durnbaugh, *To Serve the Present Age*, pp. 144–47.

32. "UNRRA and the Dunkers," *Time*, 23 July 1945, quoted in Rebecca Bushong, "Ben Bushong — Apostle of Mercy," *Brethren Life and Thought* 24 (1979): 71–88.

33. Wayne Northey, "Reconciliation," *Mennonite Encyclopedia* 5:746.

34. In the definitive Brethren resource, *Brethren Encyclopedia*, there is no article on reconciliation. Kenneth Shaffer argues that reconciliation as an act of restoring mutuality became a central element among Brethren only about 1950. As with the Mennonites there are countless examples of keeping peace or refusing to retaliate, but there are fewer instances of overcoming enmity. See Snyder and Shaffer, *Texts in Transit II*, pp. 192–95.

35. Howard Zehr, *Mediating the Victim-Offender Conflict* (Akron, Pa.: Mennonite Central Committee, n.d.), pp. 19–21.

Chapter 6 / Living in Hope

1. John S. Oyer, "Suffering," *Mennonite Encyclopedia* 5:862–63.

2. *Martyrs' Mirror*, pp. 774–75.

3. *Martyrs' Mirror*, pp. 67–68.

4. *Martyrs' Mirror*, p. 69.

5. *The Complete Writings of Menno Simons*, pp. 581–622.

6. *Ausbund, das ist: Etliche schöne Christliche Lieder* (Lancaster County, Pa.: Verlag von den Amischen Gemeinden, 1991, 13. Auflage), p. 663 (my translation).

7. John Howard Yoder has made these definitive distinctions in *Christian Witness to the State*.

8. See Michael L. Hodson, *Brethren Encyclopedia*, s.v. "Universalism"; and Williams, *Radical Reformation*, pp. 839–40.

9. *The Chronicle of the Hutterian Brethren*, p. lxv.

10. Joseph A. Amato, *Victims and Values: A History and a Theory of Suffering* (New York: Praeger, 1990), p. 210.

11. From the *Ausbund*, quoted in Ethelbert Stauffer, "The Anabaptist Theology of Martyrdom," *Mennonite Quarterly Review* 19 (1945): 179–214 (my translation).

12. Warren W. Slabaugh, *The Role of the Servant* (Elgin, Ill.: Brethren Publishing House, 1954).

13. *Die Lieder der Hutterischen Brüder* (Cayley, Alberta: Hutterischen Brüdern, 1914), p. 23 (my translation).

14. *Ausbund*, 607 (my translation).

15. Personal correspondence with Donald F. Durnbaugh, 14 June 1993.

16. In regard to birth, Jürgen Moltmann makes the distinction between vitality (biological life) and humanity (corporate life); he then carries the same distinction into his discussion of death, distinguishing between physical death and social death. He argues that we stress the physical to such an extent that we fail to help persons, and their community, in the art of surrendering life; Moltmann, *The Experiment Hope* (Philadelphia: Fortress Press, 1975), pp. 158–71. See also Paul D. Simmons, *Birth and Death: Bioethical Decision-making* (Philadelphia: Westminster Press, 1983), pp. 81–82, and, for the same distinctions from the perspective of medical anthropology, Foster and Anderson, *Medical Anthropology*, p. 299.

17. See Tilman R. Smith, "Homes, Retirement and Nursing," *Mennonite Encyclopedia* 5:390–91.

18. A. J. Metzler, "Death and Dying," *Mennonite Encyclopedia* 5:217–18.

19. Hostetler, *Hutterite Society*, pp. 247–49.

20. Mary Sue H. Rosenberger, *Caring: A History of Brethren Homes, 1889–1989* (Elgin, Ill.: Brethren Homes and Hospitals Association, 1989).

21. Hostetler, *Hutterite Society*, pp. 250–51.

22. Linda L. Fry, *Brethren Encyclopedia*, s.v. "Funerals"; John M. Janzen, "Funerals," *Mennonite Encyclopedia* 5:320.

Chapter 7 / The Vision Revisited

1. Bender, "The Anabaptist Vision."

2. Series foreword to *Believers Church Bible Commentary*. See Richard B. Gardner, *Matthew* (Scottdale, Pa.: Herald Press, 1991), p. 12.

3. Snyder, *First Corinthians*, pp. vii–viii.

4. Mennonite theologian John Howard Yoder addresses the centrality of Jesus in his book *The Politics of Jesus* (Grand Rapids, Mich.: Eerdmans, 1972), p. 23.

5. "Before Emperor Constantine, following Jesus—being Christian—meant having a visibly different way of living. It was a life modeled on Jesus." J. Denny Weaver, "Mennonite Theological Self-Understanding: A Response to A. James Reimer," in Redekop and Steiner, *Mennonite Identity*, p. 54.

6. Ramsay MacMullen, *Christianizing the Roman Empire, A.D. 100–400* (New Haven: Yale University Press, 1984).

7. Robert Thouless, *Conventionalization and Assimilation in Religious Movements as Problems in Social Psychology* (Oxford: Oxford University Press, 1940).

8. Robert Redfield, *The Little Community* (Chicago: University of Chicago Press, 1955), pp. 33–51, and *Peasant Society and Culture* (Chicago: University of Chicago Press, 1956). Although Redfield dealt primarily with rural or peasant societies, further studies by advocates of the Redfield grid indicate a similar pattern in towns and villages. In his oft-quoted introduction to the work of Horace Miner's work on St. Denis in Quebec, Redfield spells out quite clearly the nature of peasant society; see pp. xiii–xix in Miner, *St. Denis* (Chicago: University of Chicago Press, 1939). But in the revised edition Miner extends the qualities of peasant life to all human community; see Miner, *St. Denis*, rev. ed. (Chicago: University of Chicago Press, 1963), pp. v–vii, as well as the introduction to the revised edition of Miner, *The Primitive City of Timbuctoo* (Garden City, N.Y.: Doubleday, 1965), pp. xii–xiii.

9. Melford E. Spiro, *Buddhism and Society: A Great Tradition and Its Burmese Vicissitudes* (New York: Harper and Row, 1970), pp. 5, 14. Spiro makes this point even more clearly in his preface to the second edition; see Spiro, *Buddhism and Society: A Great Tradition and Its Burmese Vicissitudes*, 2d ed. (Berkeley: University of California Press, 1982), pp. xviii–xix.

10. Itumeleng Mosala, *Biblical Hermeneutics and Black Theology in South Africa* (Grand Rapids, Mich.: Eerdmans, 1989), pp. 173–89.

11. Also Luke 16:18 and Matthew 5:31–32; Mark 10:10–12 and Matthew 19:9; Hermas Mandate 4.1:6b, 10. Hermas refers to a second-century work often called *The Shepherd of Hermas*, which was popular with Christian congregations.

12. Gospel of Thomas 55:1–2a; 101; also Luke 14:25–26 and Matthew 10:37. The Gospel of Thomas is a collection of the sayings of Jesus used primarily by gnostic Christians. It has similarities with the sayings source used by Matthew and Luke. Sometimes it is considered the earliest witness to a saying of Jesus.

13. Gospel of Thomas 99; also Mark 3:19b–21, 31–35, and Matthew 12:46–50 and Luke 8:19–21.

14. Anthony J. Saldarini, "The Gospel of Matthew and the Jewish-Christian Conflict," in *Social History of the Matthean Community*, ed. David L. Balch (Minneapolis: Augsburg Fortress, 1991), p. 92.

15. 1 Corinthians 9:14; 1 Corinthians 10:27; Gospel of Thomas 14:2; Luke 10:1, 4–11, and Matthew 10:7, 10b, 12–14; Mark 6:7–13 and Matthew 10:1, 8–10a, 11, and Luke 9:1–6; Didache 11–13; 1 Timothy 5:18b. The Didache, like Hermas, was a popular document among second-century Christian congregations. It contains many sayings of Jesus probably taken from the continuing oral Jesus tradition.

16. Data taken primarily from John Dominic Crossan, *The Historical Jesus*, pp. 434–41. For the discussion on healing and eating see pp. 303–53.

17. Romans 1:3; 2 Timothy 2:8; Matthew 2:1–12; Luke 2:1–20; John 7:41–42; Ignatius Smyrna 1:1a; Ignatius Ephesians 18:2c; Ignatius Trallians 9:1a. Ignatius was

bishop of Antioch during the early years of the second century. His letters to various churches are an important resource for the post-apostolic period.

18. Gospel of Thomas 14:3; Mark 7:14–15; Matthew 15:10–11; Acts 10:14b; Acts 11:8b.

19. Gospel of Thomas 44; Luke 12:10 and Matthew 12:32a; Mark 3:28–30 and Matthew 12:31, 32b; Didache 11:7.

20. Gospel of Thomas 52; Egerton Gospel 1; John 5:39–47; John 9:29. The Egerton Gospel is a papyrus fragment first published in 1935; it contains material somewhat like the Gospel of John, but in an earlier stage.

21. Gospel of Thomas 71; Mark 14:55–59 and Matthew 26:59–61; Mark 15:29–32a, Matthew 27:39–43, and Luke 23:35–37; Acts 16:11–14; John 2:18–22.

22. 1 Thessalonians 4:13–18; Didache 16:6–8; Matthew 24:30a; Mark 13:24–27, Matthew 24:29, 30b–31, and Luke 21:25–28; Revelation 1:7; Revelation 1:13; Revelation 14:14; John 19:37.

23. 1 Corinthians 10:14–22; 1 Corinthians 11:23–25; Mark 14:22–25, Matthew 26:26–29, and Luke 22:15–19a [19b–20]; Didache 9:1–4; John 6:51b–58.

24. J. L. Houlden, *A Commentary on the Johannine Epistles* (New York: Harper and Row, 1973), p. 18.

25. Patrick Bruun, "Symboles, signes et monogrammes," *Acta instituti Romani Finlandiae* (Helsinki, 1963), 1:2, pp. 73–166.

26. For descriptions and photographs of symbols and pictures, see Graydon F. Snyder, *Ante Pacem: Archaeological Evidence of Church Life before Constantine* (Macon, Ga.: Mercer University Press, 1985).

27. Snyder, *Ante Pacem*, plate 33, p. 64 (Museo Pio cristiano, #123). In a fresco from the hypogeum of Vibia the dead person (Vibia) is being led to her proper place at the table. See James Stevenson, *The Catacombs: Life and Death in Early Christianity* (London: Thames and Hudson, 1978), p. 120.

28. Snyder, *Ante Pacem*, p. 21. It may be that the enigmatic Adam and Eve pictures also represent the yearning for nature and the land. The thesis has been proposed by L. Troje, *Adam und Zwh. Sitzungberichte Heidelberger Akademie der Wissenschaft* Phil-hist. Klasse, 1916, and Sigrid Esche, *Adam und Eva* (Düsseldorf: Schwann, 1957), pp. 30–32.

29. Snyder, *Ante Pacem*, pp. 62–63.

30. Snyder, *Ante Pacem*, pp. 122, 129. Data in J. Suolahti, P. Bruun, and H. Nordberg, "Position sociale des personnes mentionnées dans les inscriptions," *Acta instituti Romani Finlandiae* 1:2:167–87.

31. Guillermo Cook considers the first Anabaptists as primary examples of Protestant base communities. See Cook, *The Expectation of the Poor: Latin American Basic Ecclesial Communities in Protestant Perspective* (Maryknoll, N.Y.: Orbis Books, 1985), pp. 179–81.

32. Carlos Mesters claims that most base communities started from Bible "study" groups (*círculos bíblicos*); see his article "The Use of the Bible in Christian Communities of the Common People," in *The Challenge of Basic Christian Communities*, ed. Sergio Torres and John Eagleson (Maryknoll, N.Y.: Orbis Books, 1981),

pp. 197–210. Cook (*Expectation of the Poor*, pp. 178–80) claims that grass-roots communities are automatically evangelistic. Because they are formed "over against," they must enlist others. Only hierarchicalism and institutionalization will stop the growth process.

33. CEBs develop natural leaders who perform various functions. Despite the power of the priest in Latin American Catholicism, such leaders do take over some priestly functions. And many priests identify more closely with the laity. See Cook, *Expectation of the Poor*, pp. 62–63.

34. João Batista Libaño, "A Community with a New Image," *International Review of Missions* 68 (1979): 243–65.

35. Leonardo Boff, "Theological Characteristics of a Grassroots Church," in Torres and Eagleson, *Challenge of Basic Christian Communities*, pp. 124–44.

36. Hugues Portelli, *Gramsci et le bloc historique* (Paris: Presses Universitaires de France, 1972), pp. 86–89.

37. Mesters, "Use of the Bible," pp. 197–210.

Chapter 8 / Communities of Wellness

1. Mary Ann Moyer Kulp, *No Longer Strangers* (Elgin, Ill.: Brethren Press, 1968), p. 77.

2. Most of the following data were taken from Joel K. Thompson, "The Health of Lafiya," *Messenger* (1 November 1972), pp. 11–13.

3. This description is taken from Kermon Thomasson, "Lafiya Lives Up to Its Name," *Messenger* (March 1978), pp. 10–11.

4. *The Lafiya Guide: A Congregational Handbook for Whole-Person Health Ministry* (Elgin, Ill.: Association of Brethren Caregivers, 1993), p. 11.

5. *On the Way: An Introduction to Wellness* (Goshen, Ind.: Mennonite Mutual Aid, n.d.), n.p.

6. *On the Way.*

7. *Congregational Wellness Manual* (Goshen, Ind.: Mennonite Mutual Aid, 1983), p. 6.

8. *Congregational Wellness Manual*, p. 17.

9. Donald B. Ardell, *High Level Wellness: An Alternative to Doctors, Drugs, and Disease* (Emmaus, Pa.: Rodale Press, 1977).

10. *Congregational Wellness Manual*, p. 14.

11. This quotation and those that follow are taken from "Relationships, Wellness Series 8" (Goshen, Ind.: Mennonite Mutual Aid, 1983).

12. *Congregational Wellness Manual*, p. 51.

13. Snyder, *Tough Choices*, pp. 117–20.

14. In terms of the "one" and the "many," the Anabaptist sense of corporateness would mean that the individual does reflect the many or the whole. The adult individuals do not really need corporate advice or counsel. Since they were formed by the community they will act according to their community formation. But a person could reach a point in life when that formation is not clear or discernible. One might

say that just as for medieval theologians sin could cloud the image of God (reason), so for Anabaptists illness could cloud the image of God (corporate discernment).

15. "Guiding Principles for Responding to the Health Care Crisis (Mennonite Mutual Aid, 1992).

16. Developed by J. Marvin Nafziger for Mennonite Mutual Aid, Goshen, Indiana. Printed in *Congregational Wellness Manual*, p. 98.

17. Bernie Wiebe, "Health Services," *Mennonite Encyclopedia* 5:366–68.

18. Wiebe, "Health Services," p. 367. Brethren mission historian Elgin Moyer cites Brethren missionaries who felt the medical work pulled them beyond their competence and energy; Moyer, *Missions in the Church of the Brethren: Their Development and Effect upon the Denomination* (Elgin, Ill.: Brethren Publishing House, 1931), p. 217.

19. No matter how infected they may be by dissident voices, Anabaptists do know that Christianity extends by the formation of new communities and that good health will result from trusting relationships. As just one example we can note the formation of a Mennonite community in Kobe, Japan. The Japanese wished to break with existing Western patterns and put primary emphasis on relationships (*koinonia*) rather than institutional function. See Yamada Takashi, "A Young Church Leads the Way," *Mennonite Encyclopedia* 5:592. As early as 1922 the Brethren in Anklesvar, India, determined that they should train village workers who would be, of course, village teachers but who also would develop gardens, improve village sanitation and hygiene, and work for better agricultural practices; Moyer, *Missions in the Church of the Brethren*, p. 209.

Index